Selection of Barcelona and Costa Dorada Hotels and Restaurants

BERLITZ

Where do you start? Choosing a hotel or restaurant in a place you're not familiar with can be daunting. To help you find your way, we have made a selection from the *Red Guide to Spain and Portugal 1987* published by Michelin, the recognized authority on gastronomy and accommodation throughout Europe.

Our own Berlitz criteria have been price and location. In the hotel section, for a double room with bath but without breakfast, Higher-priced means above ptas. 10,000, Medium-priced ptas. 6,000–10,000, Lower-priced below ptas. 6,000. As to restaurants, for a meal consisting of a starter, a main course and a dessert, Higher-priced means above ptas. 3,500, Medium-priced ptas. 2,300–3,500, Lower-priced below ptas. 2,300. For Costa Dorada resorts, however, to avoid confusion of detail, we have simply replaced after each entry the three categories with $$$ for Higher-priced, $$ for Medium-priced and $ for Lower-priced. Special features where applicable, plus regular closing days are also given. As a general rule many Barcelona restaurants are closed in August. Hotels at Costa Dorada resorts often close during the winter season. For hotels and restaurants, check that they are open; reservations are advisable. In Spain, hotel and restaurant prices include a service charge, but 6–12% IVA will be added to the bill.

For a wider choice of hotels and restaurants, we strongly recommend you obtain the authoritative Michelin *Red Guide to Spain and Portugal,* which gives a comprehensive and reliable picture of the situation throughout these countries.

Barcelona

HOTELS

HIGHER-PRICED
(above ptas. 10,000)

Arenas
Capitán Arenas 20
08034 Barcelona
Tel. 204 03 00
Tlx. 54990
No restaurant, but evening snacks available.

Calderón
rambla Catalunya 26
08007 Barcelona
Tel. 301 00 00
Tlx. 51549
Outdoor swimming pool.

Diplomatic
Pau Claris 122
08009 Barcelona
Tel. 317 31 00
Tlx. 54701
Outdoor swimming pool. La Salsa restaurant.

Hesperia
Los Vergós 20
08017 Barcelona
Tel. 204 55 51
Tlx. 98403
Quiet hotel. Cafeteria only.

Presidente
av. de la Diagonal 570
08021 Barcelona
Tel. 200 21 11
Tlx. 52180
Outdoor swimming pool.

Ritz
Gran Via de les Corts
Catalanes 668
08010 Barcelona
Tel. 318 52 00
Tlx. 52739
Outdoor dining.

G. H. Sarriá
av. de Sarriá 50
08029 Barcelona
Tel. 239 11 09
Tlx. 51033
View.

MEDIUM-PRICED
(ptas. 6,000–10,000)

Atenas
av. Meridiana 151
08026 Barcelona
Tel. 232 20 11
Outdoor swimming pool. No restaurant, but snacks available.

Balmoral
vía Augusta 5
08006 Barcelona
Tel. 217 87 00
Tlx. 54087
Cafeteria only.

Colón
av. de la Catedral 7
08002 Barcelona
Tel. 301 14 04
Tlx. 52654

Condado
Aribau 201
08021 Barcelona
Tel. 200 23 11
Tlx. 54546

Covadonga
av. de la Diagonal 596
08021 Barcelona
Tel. 209 55 11
Cafeteria only.

Derby
Loreto 21
08029 Barcelona
Tel. 322 32 15
Tlx. 97429
No restaurant.

Expo Hotel
Mallorca 1
08014 Barcelona
Tel. 325 12 12
Tlx. 54147
Outdoor swimming pool.
Self-service cafeteria only.

Gala Placidia
vía Augusta 112
08006 Barcelona
Tel. 217 82 00
Tlx. 98820

Gotico
Jaime 1-14
08002 Barcelona
Tel. 315 22 11
Tlx. 97206
No restaurant.

Mitre
Bertrán 15
08023 Barcelona
Tel. 212 11 04
Tlx. 51531
No restaurant.

Numancia
Numancia 74
08029 Barcelona
Tel. 322 44 51
Cafeteria only.

Pedralbes
Fontcuberta 4
08007 Barcelona
Tel. 203 71 12
Tlx. 52925
Cafeteria only.

Regente
rambla de Catalunya 76
08008 Barcelona
Tel. 215 25 70
Tlx. 51939
Outdoor swimming pool.

Regina
Vergara 2
08002 Barcelona
Tel. 301 32 32
Tlx. 59380
No restaurant, but snacks available.

Rialto
Fernando 42
08002 Barcelona
Tel. 318 52 12
Tlx. 097206
Cafeteria only.

Royal
Ramblas 117
08002 Barcelona

Tel. 301 94 00
Tlx. 97565
No restaurant.

Wilson
av. de la Diagonal 568
08021 Barcelona
Tel. 209 25 11
Tlx. 54134
No restaurant.

LOWER-PRICED
(below ptas. 6,000)

Bonanova Park
Capitán Arenas 51
08034 Barcelona
Tel. 204 09 00
Tlx. 54990
No restaurant.

Cortés
Santa Ana 25
08002 Barcelona
Tel. 317 91 12
Tlx. 98215

Las Corts
Travessera de Les Corts 292
08029 Barcelona
Tel. 322 08 11
Tlx. 59001
No restaurant, but snacks available.

Lleó
Pelai 24
08001 Barcelona
Tel. 318 13 12
Tlx. 98338

Regencia Colón
Sagristans 13
08002 Barcelona
Tel. 318 98 58; Tlx. 98175
No restaurant.

San Agustin
pl. Sant Agustin 3
08001 Barcelona
Tel. 317 28 82; Tlx. 98121

Torelló
Ample 31
08002 Barcelona
Tel. 315 40 11; Tlx. 54606
No restaurant.

RESTAURANTS

HIGHER-PRICED
(above ptas. 3,500)

Alberto
Ganduxer 50
08021 Barcelona
Tel. 201 00 09
Outdoor dining. Closed Sunday evening.

Ara-Cata
Dr. Ferràn 33
08034 Barcelona
Tel. 204 10 53
Notably good cuisine. Closed Saturday.

Azulete
vía Augusta 281
08017 Barcelona
Tel. 203 59 43
Notably good cuisine. Outdoor dining. Flowered terrace. Closed Saturday lunchtime and Sunday.

Bel Air
Córcega 286
08008 Barcelona
Tel. 237 75 88
Rice specialities. Closed Sunday.

Beltxenea
Mallorca 275
08008 Barcelona
Tel. 215 30 24
Outdoor dining. Terrace.
Closed Saturday lunchtime and
Sunday.

Botafumeiro
Major de Grácia 81
08012 Barcelona
Tel. 218 42 30
Notably good cuisine. Seafood
specialities. Closed Sunday eve-
ning and Monday.

El Dento
Loreto 32
08029 Barcelona
Tel. 321 67 56
Seafood specialities. Closed
Saturday.

Eldorado Petit
Dolors Monserdá 51
08017 Barcelona
Tel. 204 51 53
Notably good cuisine. Pleasant
terrace. Closed Sunday.

Neichel
av. de Pedralbes 16 bis
08034 Barcelona
Tel. 203 84 08
Excellent cuisine. Closed
Sunday.

Reno
Tuset 27
08006 Barcelona
Tel. 200 91 29
Elegant, classic restaurant.
Notably good cuisine.

Roig Robi
Séneca 20
08006 Barcelona
Tel. 218 92 22
Outdoor dining. Closed Sunday.

Vía Veneto
Ganduxer 10
08021 Barcelona
Tel. 200 72 44
Belle Epoque restaurant. Notably
good cuisine.

MEDIUM-PRICED
(ptas. 2,300–3,500)

Agut d'Avignon
Trinidad 3 (Avinyó 8)
08002 Barcelona
Tel. 302 60 34
Typical local decor.

Aitor
Carbonnell 5
08003 Barcelona
Tel. 319 94 88
Basque cuisine. Closed Sunday.

Alt Berlin
Diagonal 633
08028 Barcelona
Tel. 339 01 66
German cuisine.

Azpiolea
Casanova 167
08036 Barcelona
Tel. 230 90 30
Basque cuisine. Closed Sunday evening.

La Balsa
Infanta Isabel 4
08022 Barcelona
Tel. 211 50 48
Outdoor dining. Closed Sunday and Monday lunchtime.

Brasserie Flo
Junqueras 10
08003 Barcelona
Tel. 317 80 37

Can Solé
San Carlos 4
08003 Barcelona
Tel. 319 50 12
Seafood specialities. Closed Sunday.

Los Caracoles
Escudillers 14
08002 Barcelona
Tel. 301 20 41
Typical restaurant decorated in regional country style.

Chévere
rambla del Prat 14
08012 Barcelona
Tel. 217 03 59
Closed Saturday lunchtime and Sunday.

La Cuineta
Paradís 4
08002 Barcelona
Tel. 315 01 11

Typical restaurant, tastefully installed in a 17th-century "bodega". Closed Monday.

Font del Gat
passeig Santa Madrona, Montjuic
08004 Barcelona
Tel. 224 02 24
Outdoor dining. Typical local decor.

Gorria
Diputació 421
08013 Barcelona
Tel. 245 11 64
Basque-Navarre cuisine. Closed Sunday.

El Gran Café
Avinyó 9
08002 Barcelona
Tel. 318 79 86
Piano music in the evening. 1900s-style restaurant. Closed Sunday.

Hostal del Sol
piso 1, passeig de Gràcia 44
08007 Barcelona
Tel. 215 62 25
Piano music in the evening.

Hostal Sant Jordi
Travessera de Dalt 123
08024 Barcelona
Tel. 213 10 37
Closed Sunday evening.

Las Indias
passeig Manuel Girona 38 bis
08034 Barcelona
Tel. 204 48 00
Closed Sunday evening.

Jaume de Provença
Provença 88
08029 Barcelona
Tel. 230 00 29
Notably good cuisine. Modern restaurant. Closed Sunday evening and Monday.

Lagunak
Berlín 19
08014 Barcelona
Tel. 322 12 56
Basque-Navarre cuisine. Closed Sunday.

Llúria
Roger de Llúria 23
08010 Barcelona
Tel. 301 74 94
Closed Sunday.

A la Menta
passeig Manuel Girona 50
08034 Barcelona
Tel. 204 15 49
Typical local taverne. Closed Sunday evening. Reservation essential.

La Odisea
Copons 7
08002 Barcelona
Tel. 302 36 92
Notably good cuisine. Piano music in the evening. Closed Saturday lunchtime and Sunday.

Pá i Trago
Parlamento 41
08015 Barcelona
Tel. 241 13 20
Typical local restaurant. Closed Monday.

A'Palloza
Casanova 42
08011 Barcelona
Tel. 253 17 86
Seafood specialities. Closed Sunday.

La Senyora Grill
Bori i Fontesta 45
08017 Barcelona
Tel. 201 25 77
Outdoor dining.

El Trapio
Esperanza 25
08017 Barcelona
Tel. 211 58 17
Outdoor dining. Closed Sunday evening and Monday.

La Venta
pl. Dr. Andreu
08022 Barcelona
Tel. 212 64 55
Old café. Outdoor dining. Closed Sunday.

Outskirts of Barcelona

Casa Quirze
Laureano Miró 202
08950 Esplugues de Llobregat
Tel. 371 10 84
Closed Sunday evening and Monday.

La Masía
av. Paisos Catalans 58
08950 Esplugues de Llobregat
Tel. 371 37 42
Outdoor dining on terrace beneath the pines.

LOWER-PRICED
(below ptas. 2,300)

L'Alberg
Ramón y Cajal 13
08012 Barcelona
Tel. 214 10 25
Typical restaurant with country decor.

Barceloneta
paseo Nacional 70
08003 Barcelona
Tel. 319 43 05
Outdoor dining.

Bel Cavalletto
Santaló 125
08021 Barcelona
Tel. 201 79 11

Can Culleretes
Quintana 5
08002 Barcelona
Tel. 317 64 85
Typical local restaurant. Closed Sunday evening and Monday.

Julivert Meu
Jorge Girona Salgado 12
08034 Barcelona
Tel. 204 11 96

L'Olivé
Muntaner 171
08036 Barcelona
Tel. 230 90 27
Outdoor dining. Typical local restaurant. Reservation essential.

El Patí Blau
Jorge Girona Salgado 14
08034 Barcelona
Tel. 204 22 15

7 Puertas
passeig d'Isabel 11-14
08003 Barcelona
Tel. 319 30 33
Piano music in the evening.

Outskirts of Barcelona

Can Cortés
urbanización Ciudad Condal
Tibidabo, on Sant Cugat del Vallés highway
08023 Barcelona
Tel. 674 17 04
View. Outdoor dining. Catalan wine bar. Old "masia". Outdoor swimming pool (small fee).

Costa Dorada and Inland Resorts

CALAFELL

Hotels

Canadá $
av. Mosén Jaime Soler 44
43820 Calafell
Tel. (977) 69 15 00
Outdoor dining. Outdoor swimming pool. Hotel tennis court.

Kursaal $$
av. San Juan de Dios 119
43820 Calafell
Tel. (977) 69 23 00
Quiet hotel. View. Outdoor dining.

Restaurants

La Barca Ca L'Ardet $$
av. San Juan de Dios 79
43820 Calafell
Tel. (977) 69 15 59
Outdoor dining. Seafood specialities. Closed Wednesday.

O Braseiro Galaico $
Marta Moraga 29
43882 Segur de Calafell
Tel. (977) 69 20 33
Closed Tuesday.

CAMBRILS

Hotels

Can Solé $
Ramón Llull 19
43850 Cambrils
Tel. (977) 36 02 36
Outdoor dining.

Mónica H. $
Galcerán Marquet 3
43850 Cambrils
Tel. (977) 36 01 16
Lawn with palm trees. Garden.

Princep $
pl. de la Iglesia 2
43850 Cambrils
Tel. (977) 36 11 27

Rovira $
av. Diputación 6
43850 Cambrils
Tel. (977) 36 09 00
View. Outdoor dining.

Tropicana $
av. Diputación
43850 Cambrils
Tel. (977) 36 01 12
Outdoor dining. Outdoor swimming pool. Garden.

Restaurants

El Caliu $$
Pau Casals 22
43850 Cambrils
Tel. (977) 36 01 08
Country-style decor. Outdoor dining. Meat prepared on a grill. Closed Sunday evening and Monday.

Can Bosch $$
rambla Jaime 1-19
43850 Cambrils
Tel. (977) 36 00 19
Notably good cuisine. Seafood specialities. Outdoor dining. Closed Sunday evening and Monday.

Can Gatell $$
paseo Miramar 27
43850 Cambrils
Tel. (977) 36 01 06
Notably good cuisine. Seafood specialities. Outdoor dining. View. Closed Monday evening, Tuesday out of season and Tuesday and Wednesday lunchtime in summer.

Casa Gallau $$
Pescadores 25
43850 Cambrils
Tel. (977) 36 02 61
Outdoor dining. Seafood specialities. Closed Wednesday evening and Thursday.

Casa Gatell $$$
paseo Miramar 26
43850 Cambrils
Tel. (977) 36 00 57
Notably good cuisine. Seafood
specialities. Outdoor dining. View.
Closed Sunday evening and Mon-
day.

Eugenia $$
Consolat de Mar 80
43850 Cambrils
Tel. (977) 36 01 68
Notably good cuisine. Seafood
specialities. Outdoor dining.
Terrace with flowers. Closed
Tuesday evening and Wednesday.

Marina $$
paseo Miramar 42
43850 Cambrils
Tel. (977) 36 04 32
View. Outdoor dining. Closed
Thursday.

Mas Gallau $$
on highway N 340
apartado 129 Cambrils
Tel. (977) 36 05 88
Country-style decor.

Pizzería Roma $
pl. Cataluña 2
43850 Cambrils
Tel. (977) 36 10 46
Outdoor dining. Italian cuisine.
Closed Monday.

Rovira Antiguo $$
paseo Miramar 37
43850 Cambrils
Tel. (977) 36 01 05
View. Outdoor dining. Seafood
specialities.

CASTELLDEFELS

Hotels

Elvira $
calle 22 de la Pineda 13
08860 Castelldefels
Tel. (93) 665 15 50
Set among the pines. Outdoor
swimming pool.

Luna $$
paseo de la Marina 155
08860 Castelldefels
Tel. (93) 665 21 50
Tlx. 97710
Outdoor swimming pool.
Garden.

Mediterráneo $
paseo Marítimo 294
08860 Castelldefels
Tel. (93) 665 21 00
Tlx. 93503
Outdoor swimming pool.

Neptuno $
paseo Garbi 74
08860 Castelldefels
Tel. (93) 665 14 50
Set among the pine trees.
Outdoor dining. Outdoor swim-
ming pool. Garden. Hotel tennis
court.

G. H. Rey Don Jaime $$$
Torre Barona
08860 Castelldefels
Tel. (93) 665 13 00
Tlx. 50151
Quiet hotel. Outdoor dining. Out-
door swimming pool. Garden.
Hotel tennis court.

Riviera $
on highway C 246
08860 Castelldefels
Tel. (93) 665 14 00

Restaurants

La Bonne Table $$
on highway C 246
08860 Castelldefels
Tel. (93) 665 37 55
Outdoor dining. French cuisine.
Closed Tuesday.

Las Botas $$
on highway C 246
08860 Castelldefels
Tel. (93) 665 18 24
Outdoor dining. Typical decor.
Closed Sunday evening.

La Canasta $$
pl. del Mar 3
08860 Castelldefels
Tel. (93) 665 68 57
Outdoor dining. Closed Tuesday.

COMARRUGA

Hotels

Casa Martí $
Vilafranca 8
43880 Comarruga
Tel. (977) 68 01 11
Quiet hotel. View. Outdoor
swimming pool. Hotel tennis
court.

G. H. Europe $$
vía Palfuriana 107
43880 Comarruga
Tel. (977) 68 04 11
Tlx. 56681
View. Outdoor dining. Heated
outdoor swimming pool. Hotel
tennis court.

Restaurants

Els Pins $
paseo Marítimo 77
43880 Comarruga
Tel. (977) 68 05 05
View. Outdoor dining.

HOSPITALET DEL INFANTE

Hotels

Infante $
Del Mar 24
43890 Hospitalet del Infante
Tel. (977) 82 30 00
Quiet hotel. View. Outdoor
dining. Outdoor swimming pool.
Hotel tennis court.

Tropicana $
carret. N 340
43892 Miami Playa
Tel. (977) 81 03 40
Outdoor swimming pool.

Restaurants

Les Barques $$
Comandante Gimeno 21
43890 Hospitalet del Infante
Tel. (977) 82 39 61
View. Seafood specialities. Closed
Tuesday October to March.

MONTSERRAT

Hotels

Albat Cisneros $
pl. Monasterio
08691 Montserrat
Tel. (93) 835 02 01
Quiet hotel.

Monestir $
pl. Monasterio
08691 Montserrat
Tel. (93) 835 02 01
Quiet hotel. No restaurant.

Restaurants

Montserrat $$
pl. Apostols
08691 Montserrat
Tel. (93) 835 02 51 (ext. 165)
View. Lunch only.

Santa Cecilia $
on Casa Masana highway
08691 Montserrat
Tel. (93) 835 03 09
*View. Outdoor dining. Closed
Thursday except July and August.*

SALOU

Hotels

Carabela Roc $
Pau Casals 108
43840 Salou
Tel. (977) 37 01 66
Tlx. 56709
*Beneath the pine trees. View. No
restaurant.*

Planas $
pl. Bonet 3
43840 Salou
Tel. (977) 38 01 08
Outdoor dining. Terrace.

Restaurants

Can Costa $
Pau Casals 78
43840 Salou
Tel. (977) 37 04 57
Outdoor dining.

Casa Font $$
Colón 17, Edificio Els Pilons
43840 Salou
Tel. (977) 38 57 45
View. Outdoor dining.

Casa Soler $$
Virgen del Carmen
43840 Salou
Tel. (977) 38 04 63
Outdoor dining.

La Goleta $$
Gavina - playa Capellans
43840 Salou
Tel. (977) 38 35 66
View. Outdoor dining.

Macarrilla $$
paseo Jaime 1 - 24
43840 Salou
Tel. (977) 38 54 15
Outdoor dining. Closed Tuesday.

Reymar $$
pl. Manuel de Falla 2
43000 Tarragona - apartado 16
Tel. (977) 37 04 90
*Beneath the pine trees. View.
Outdoor dining.*

SITGES

Hotels

Antemare $$
Verge de Montserrat 48
08870 Sitges
Tel. (93) 894 06 00
Tlx. 52962
Quiet hotel. Outdoor dining. Outdoor swimming pool.

Calípolis $$
passeig Maritim
08870 Sitges
Tel. (93) 894 15 00
Tlx. 53067
View. Outdoor dining. La Brasa grill.

Galeón $
San Francisco 44
08870 Sitges
Tel. (93) 894 06 12
Outdoor swimming pool.

Los Pinos $$
passeig Maritim
08870 Sitges
Tel. (93) 894 15 50
Tlx. 52962
View. Outdoor swimming pool.

Platjador $
passeig de la Ribera 35
08870 Sitges
Tel. (93) 894 50 54

La Reserva $
passeig Maritim 62
08870 Sitges
Tel. (93) 894 18 33
Quiet hotel. View. Outdoor dining. Garden planted with trees.

Romantic y la Renaixença $
Sant Isidre 33
08870 Sitges
Tel. (93) 894 06 43
Tlx. 52962
No restaurant. Patio-garden planted with trees.

Terramar $$
passeig Maritim 30
08870 Sitges
Tel. (93) 894 00 50
Tlx. 53186
Quiet hotel. View. Outdoor dining. Outdoor swimming pool. Garden. Tennis court.

Restaurants

Els 4 Gats $
San Pablo 13
08870 Sitges
Tel. (93) 894 19 15
Closed Wednesday.

Fragata $$
passeig de la Ribera 1
08870 Sitges
Tel. (93) 894 10 86
Outdoor dining.

Mare Nostrum $$
passeig de la Ribera 60
08870 Sitges
Tel. (93) 894 33 93
Outdoor dining. Closed Wednesday.

La Masía $$
paseo Vilanova 164
08870 Sitges
Tel. (93) 894 10 76
Outdoor dining. Country-style regional decor.

14

Ródenas $$
Isla de Cuba 8
08870 Sitges
Tel. (93) 894 44 01
Closed Wednesday.

Vivero $$
passeig Balmins
08870 Sitges
Tel. (93) 894 21 49
*View. Outdoor dining. Seafood
specialities. Closed Tuesday
December to May.*

TARRAGONA

Hotels

Astari $
via Augusta 95
43003 Tarragona
Tel. (977) 23 69 00
*View. Outdoor dining. Outdoor
swimming pool. Garden.*

Lauria $
rambla Nova 20
43004 Tarragona
Tel. (977) 23 67 12
*No restaurant. Outdoor swimming
pool.*

Paris $
Maragall 4
43003 Tarragona
Tel. (977) 23 60 12
No restaurant.

Urbis $
Reding 20 bis
43001 Tarragona
Tel. (977) 21 01 16
No restaurant.

La Galería $
Rambla Nova 16
43004 Tarragona
Tel. (977) 22 82 69
*Closed Sunday evening and
Wednesday.*

Lauria 2 $$
piso 1, rambla Nova 20
43004 Tarragona
Tel. (977) 23 21 16

Mesón del Mar $$
on Barcelona highway
playa Larga
43007 Tarragona
Tel. (977) 23 94 01
*View. Outdoor dining. Closed
Sunday evening and Tuesday.*

La Puda $$
muelle Pescadores 25
43004 Tarragona
Tel. (977) 21 15 11
Seafood specialities.

La Rambla $$
rambla Nova 10
43004 Tarragona
Tel. (977) 23 87 29
Outdoor dining.

Sol Ric $$
vía Augusta 227
43007 Tarragona
Tel. (977) 23 20 32
*Notably good cuisine. Outdoor
dining. Country-style decor.
Terrace planted with trees.*

Trabadoira $
Apodaca 7
43004 Tarragona
Tel. (977) 21 00 27
Seafood specialities. Closed Sunday evening.

TORTOSA

Hotels

Berenguer IV $
Cervantes 23
43500 Tortosa
Tel. (977) 44 08 16
Cafeteria only.

Parador Nacional Castillo de la Zuda $$
43500 Tortosa
Tel. (977) 44 44 50
Quiet hotel. View. Outdoor swimming pool. Garden.

Tortosa Parc $
Conde de Bañuelos 10
43500 Tortosa
Tel. (977) 44 61 12
No restaurant.

VILLANUEVA Y GELTRÚ

Hotels

César $
Isaac Peral 4
08800 Villanueva y Geltrú
Tel. (93) 815 11 25
Quiet hotel. Terrace planted with trees. La Fitorra restaurant.

Solvi 70 $
paseo Ribes Roges 1
08800 Villanueva y Geltrú
Tel. (93) 815 12 45
View.

Restaurants

Chez Bernard et Marguerite $$
Ramón Llull 4
08800 Villanueva y Geltrú
Tel. (93) 815 56 04
French cuisine. Outdoor dining.

Cossetania $$
passeig Maritim 92
08800 Villanueva y Geltrú
Tel. (93) 815 55 59
Outdoor dining. Seafood specialities. Closed Wednesday.

Peixerot $$
passeig Maritim 56
08800 Villanueva y Geltrú
Tel. (93) 815 06 25
Outdoor dining. Seafood specialities. Closed Sunday evening except in summer.

Pere Peral $$
Isaac Peral 15
08800 Villanueva y Geltrú
Tel. (93) 815 29 96
Outdoor dining. Terrace beneath the pine trees. Closed Monday.

El Pescador $
passeig del Carme 45
08800 Villanueva y Geltrú
Tel. (93) 815 31 42
Outdoor dining. Seafood specialities.

BERLITZ®

BARCELONA and COSTA DORADA

1988/1989 Edition

By the staff of Berlitz Guides
A Macmillan Company

8th Printing
1988/1989 Edition

How to use our guide

- All the practical information, hints and tips that you will need before and during the trip start on page 98.

- For general background, see the sections Barcelona and the Costa Dorada, p. 6, and A Brief History, p. 10.

- All the sights to see are listed between pages 17 and 70. Our own choice of sights most highly recommended is pinpointed by the Berlitz traveller symbol.

- Entertainment, nightlife and all other leisure activities are described from pages 71 to 83 and 92 to 97, while information on restaurants and cuisine is to be found between pages 84 and 91.

- Finally, there is an index at the back of the book, pp. 126–128.

Although we make every effort to ensure the accuracy of all the information in this book, changes occur incessantly. We cannot therefore take responsibility for facts, prices, addresses and circumstances in general that are constantly subject to alteration. Our guides are updated on a regular basis as we reprint, and we are always grateful to readers who let us know of any errors, changes or serious omissions they come across.

Text: Ken Bernstein
Photography: Ken Welsh; cover: SPECTRUM COLOUR LIBRARY, London
We wish to thank Joanna Pencarska and Toni Fernandez, and the Spanish National Tourist Office, particularly Miss Mercedes Martín Bartolomé, for their valuable assistance.
Cartography: Falk-Verlag, Hamburg

Contents

Cover photo: Columbus Monument; photo pp. 2–3: View from Parc Güell.

Barcelona and the Costa Dorada

The fine golden sand which gave the Costa Dorada its name extends almost without a break along more than 150 miles of this calm Mediterranean shore.

Technically it starts north of Barcelona at the River Tordera, at the point where the more famous Costa Brava ends, and runs down, including as it goes the Costa del Maresme, to Barcelona. South of Barcelona, it begins again and stretches all the way down the coast of Catalonia to the delta of the mighty River Ebro. The Costa Dorada encompasses the great city of Barcelona and fishing villages too obscure to rate a post office. All along the coast, the swimming, boating and a bustling outdoor life continue uninterrupted under the dependable Spanish sun —until the moon and stars take over with the nightlife.

Sheer holiday fun is just one part of the Costa Dorada's invitation. This is a land of magnificent ancient churches and castles. Inland, beyond the vineyards, you can visit the

Ebro

Cambrils   Tarragona

St. Carles de la Rápita

Vilanova i la Geltrú

N

COSTA DORADA

unique mountain monastery of Montserrat—or less celebrated but unsurpassed treasures of architecture and faith. And wherever you may find yourself along the Costa Dorada, you'll sense the dynamism of Catalonia.

Spaniards in general may cherish their siesta, but the Catalan people can take it or (like the big department stores) leave it. Most Spaniards keep their women at home; in Catalonia, women enter the professions and direct traffic. Spaniards may dance the fiery flamenco; Catalans hold hands for the stately, measured *sardana*.

The people are bilingual. They speak Catalan, a derivative of Latin, as well as (and often better than) the official language of Spain, Castilian. They are more adept with foreign languages than other Spaniards. In the Middle Ages, the Catalans ruled a great sweep of the Mediterranean, including at one time or another Sicily, Sardinia, Corsica and parts of Greece. The language and culture which flourished in those imperial times still bind the Barcelona industrialist to the Sant Pol fisherman and the Amposta rice farmer.

Modern Catalonia has produced an inordinately bounti-

ful crop of original artists, such as Joan Miró and Salvador Dalí and, something of an adopted son, Picasso. But centuries earlier, brilliant Catalan architects designed stunning Romanesque churches, decorated with frescoes full of colour. With a bit of time, a tourist can see the best of everything, ancient and modern, either housed in the superlative museums of Barcelona or on the spot.

The metropolis of Catalonia, Barcelona, is a vital and very European city of flower stalls and tree-lined boulevards. The glory of its medieval architecture complements the audacity of its modern buildings. The citizens, renowned for their industriousness, work hard in 19th-century factories with huge brick chimney-stacks, or on the docks, or behind the counters of a proliferation of banks. They read more books, see more operas, and cling even more fiercely to their old traditions than the people of any other Spanish city.

The other major coastal city, Tarragona, was a provincial capital of imperial Rome. Imaginative landscaping and dramatic floodlighting at night enliven its archaeological splendours. And, in a city said to have been converted to Christianity by St. Paul himself, the cathedral—begun in the 12th century—fills the visitor with a sense of awe.

On the political map of Spain, the Costa Dorada belongs to Barcelona and Tarragona provinces. (Lleida and Girona are Catalonia's other two provinces.) In this important wine-producing district, the carafe on your table will probably be a tasty local vintage. Fishing is also a big industry, so you can be certain of fresh-from-the-net seafood. Other principal industrial activities are textile manufacture and—obviously—tourism.

The Catalans may be realists and individualists, but they are wild about singing in choirs and playing in bands and dancing the graceful *sardana*. A more eccentric aspect of their folklore is an earnest enthusiasm for climbing upon each others' shoulders to create dangerously swaying pyramids. Teams of trained castle-makers *(castellers)* travel the countryside for contests; the newspapers run articles; and, of course, the peculiar music of Catalan woodwind instruments accompanies each climax.

You'll like the cooking. From typical Catalan farm soup (loaded with sausage, beans, and a slice of meat-loaf) to nuts (local almonds, of course), the food is good and wholesome.

And before your holiday ends, you'll want to squeeze in some shopping. Local artisans and regional factories produce gifts and souvenirs both corny and sophisticated, shockingly cheap or, alas, hopelessly expensive. In a word, something for every taste.

In a Barcelona square, Catalans hold hands to dance the sardana.

A Brief History

Catalonia's long road from colony to imperial power and back to provincial status zigzags through extremes of idealism and cruelty, triumph and disaster. Characters as colourful as the Caesars, Charlemagne, and Ferdinand and Isabella left their mark on its history.

So did a 9th-century warrior named Wilfred the Hairy (Wifredo el Velloso), Catalonia's first-ever hero, who threw his noble if shaggy support behind a Frankish king called Charles the Bald. Charles was trying to expel the Moors, a recurring project in the Middle Ages. When Hairy Wilfred fell wounded, the legend goes, the king asked what reward he desired. The request—independence for Barcelona—was granted. The year was 878. But to begin at the beginning takes us far into prehistoric times. Paleolithic and Neolithic relics have turned up in Catalonia. While little is known of those early people, we are however sure that Phoenicians and Greeks brought commerce and culture to Catalonia; and the Carthaginians are said to have given Barcelona its original name, Barcino, in honour of General Hamilcar Barca, father of the legendary Hannibal.

In the 2nd Punic War (3rd century B.C.), the Romans defeated Carthage and ruled Iberia for the next six centuries. Spain gave birth to four Roman emperors. One of the capitals of the Roman empire was Tarragona, then called Tarraco. All over Catalonia, from the seashore to lonely mountaintops, the stamp of Rome remains: walls and roadways, villas and monuments, vineyards and the Catalan language, an expressive descendant of Latin.

By the 5th century A.D., Rome's grip had slackened and Spain was overrun by Vandals and Visigoths. The next in-

10

Aqueduct near Tarragona recalls Catalonia's role in Roman empire.

vasion began in 711, when Moorish forces from Africa assailed the Iberian peninsula. Muslim civilization was imposed, but the Christian efforts to reconquer Spain never ceased. The subsequent Moorish influence on Christian Spanish art and architecture, was, nonetheless, profound.

An early but indecisive defeat of the Moors was the recapture of Barcelona by Charlemagne's forces. Catalonia paid generously for its liberation, becoming a Frankish dependency called the Spanish March. Then came our heroic Count Wilfred the Hairy, who earned Barcelona its freedom.

Catalonia's Golden Age

In the Middle Ages, Catalonia prospered commercially, poli-

tically and intellectually. Count Ramón Berenguer I of Barcelona drew up a sort of constitution, the *Usatges,* in 1060. Ramón Berenguer III (1096–1131) turned Catalonia towards imperial enterprises; he formed a union with an independent Provence (the languages are very similar) and established trade relations with Italy. Ramón Berenguer IV (1131–62) married a princess of Aragon, a brilliant expansionist tactic which created a joint kingdom of great substance. The count of Barcelona became king of Aragon, and "greater Catalonia" flourished.

Jaime I (James the Conqueror) dislodged the Moors from their stubborn hold on the Balearic Islands, installing in their stead Christianity and Catalan law. His son, Pedro III the Great, through military action and a few twists of fate, added the throne of Sicily to the dynasty's collection. By the 14th century, Catalonia's fortunes had soared to breathtaking heights, with the addition of two dukedoms in Greece, the seizure of Sardinia, and the annexation of Corsica. For a time the kingdom of Catalonia was Power No. 1 in the entire Mediterranean.

This was the era, too, of great art and architecture—original designs for churches with vast naves and tall, slim columns and the striking sculptures and paintings which glorified them. And this was a heyday for the language. Ramón Llull of Majorca (1235–1315), known as Raimundus Lullus in Latin, saint and scholar, enhanced medieval culture in

Catalan. At the same time, Catalonian cartographers, especially Majorcans, were drawing the maps that were to guide the first great navigators on their journeys beyond the known horizon.

The next Catalonian figure to make history was Ferdinand (Ferran II in Catalan), who married Isabella of Castile and became Ferdinand V of Spain.

ages of discovery proved disastrous for Catalonia. The Mediterranean lost much of its importance as a trading zone, while the south-western ports of Cadiz and Seville won the franchise for the rich trans-atlantic business.

Giant effigies (opposite) *honour Ferdinand and Isabella. In Barcelona port, a replica of Columbus' ship.*

Ferdinand and Isabella, known as the Catholic Monarchs, conquered the last Moorish bastion, Granada. They also took joint credit for two other big events in 1492: they ordered the expulsion of Spain's Jews, and they sponsored Columbus on his voyage of discovery to America. Ironically, the Columbus project and other voy-

Times of Troubles

Seventeenth-century Catalonia was a troubled land, rebelling against Philip IV of Spain, putting itself under the protection of the king of France. Violent struggles went on for a dozen years. Finally a besieged Barcelona surrendered. Catalonia renewed its allegiance to the Spanish crown, but man- **13**

aged to preserve its treasured local laws.

But all was lost in the War of the Spanish Succession, in which Catalonia again demonstrated its marked difference from the rest of Spain and joined the wrong side. With the triumph of the Bourbon king Philip V in 1714, Barcelona was overrun. Official punishment followed, including the dismissal of the Catalonian parliament and the banning of the Catalan language from official use. Striking historical parallels were to follow the Spanish Civil War of 1936–39.

In the second half of the 18th century, Charles III—usually characterized as an enlightened despot—rescued Catalonia from its slump, opening up the region's ports to the very profitable Latin-American trade. He also had a visionary idea for a superport on the edge of the Ebro Delta, but the metropolis of Sant Carles de la Rápita (see page 63) never amounted to much more than an extravagant mirage.

For Catalonia as well as the rest of Spain, the 19th century seemed to be just one war after another, starting with the War of the Third Coalition in 1805 and ending with the Spanish-American War of 1898. Both were disasters. In the first, the British, under Nelson, destroyed the Spanish and French fleets at Trafalgar. In the last, Spain lost its key remaining colonies—Cuba, Puerto Rico and the Philippines.

Lauros-Giraudon

After finding America, Columbus sailed triumphantly to Barcelona.

Thirty-three years after the empire faded away, King Alfonso XIII went into exile, as Republicans gained control in several Spanish cities. National elections later in 1931 favoured the Republicans, who advocated socialist and anti-clerical policies. As conservative resistance began to crystallize, Catalonia was proclaimed an autonomous republic.

The Civil War

But confusion and disorder were growing in Spain. The conflict between left and right became more irreconcilable. Spain's youngest general, Francisco Franco, came to the head of a military insurrection. The whole world watched the three-year struggle; outside forces helped to prolong it.

Military reverses forced the Republicans to move their capital from Valencia to Barcelona in late 1937 where there had already been an outbreak of bitter fighting between two factions of the Republican side, Anarchists and Communists. There followed repeated bombings of Barcelona by Italian planes based on Majorca and a year of hardship for the population. The city fell at last in January, 1939, and Catalonia was reabsorbed into Spain—four provinces out of the nation's 50. Within two months the Civil War was over. It had cost the lives of hundreds of thousands of Spaniards.

Modern Times

Spain was able to stay neutral in the Second World War. In the postwar years, the tough law-and-order regime of Franco set in motion the nation's recovery. Then came the phenomenon of mass tourism, with profound effects on the economy and the people.

Franco's designated successor, the grandson of Alfonso XIII, was enthroned on the death of the dictator in 1975. To the dismay of Franco's followers, King Juan Carlos I flung open the gates to full parliamentary democracy. In the flush of freedom, old and new problems competed for attention. After the years of repression, the languages and cultures of Catalonia and the Basque Country flourished anew, and regional autonomy was granted.

Firmly back in the mainstream after its long isolation, democratic Spain hitched its hopes to the European Community.

Where to Go

no longer sprawling suburbs, have self-contained identities. The beaches go on for mile after mile of ideal sand and clear sea, with impressive mountains in the distance. Every fifth hilltop seems to be occupied by a castle or at least a medieval watch-tower. These relics are so common that only the best preserved or most historic are signposted.

The Coast North of Barcelona

The Costa Brava is known for its rugged cliffs and small inlets, but the Costa Dorada is downright cowardly. Rarely is the lie of the land more daring than a few miles of broad sand beaches nuzzling against a clear, gentle sea.

Let's begin by a survey of the coastline, first heading north-east from Barcelona up to the Costa Brava frontier. Technically, this stretch of the coast between Barcelona and Blanes is known as the Costa del Maresme (*maresme* meaning a low-lying coastal region susceptible to flooding).

The voyage starts with BADALONA (population 230,000), a last reminder of big-city rush and industrial necessities.

Beyond Badalona the countryside gradually takes on a more rural cast. The towns,

Costa Dorada consists of miles of lazy beaches interspersed with towns as fair as Sitges (opposite).

The first real beach centres, in a countryside noted for flower-growing, are EL MASNOU and PREMIÁ DE MAR. These beaches run right alongside the railway line. **17**

COSTA DORADA

This was the first railway in Spain, built under British technical direction and inaugurated in 1848 between Barcelona and MATARÓ, now an industrial city of about 100,000. It's all work and no play in Mataró; a tourist with a tan attracts stares from the pale local residents. Mataró was called Iluro by the ancient Romans, who left many priceless sculptures and mosaics. Most of these archaeological finds went into the municipal museum, which was shut down in 1975 when more than 200 items were found to be missing. The museum curator resigned.

CALDETES, also known as Caldes d'Estrac, is an appealing old town with villas set among the pines on its hillsides. The Romans bathed in its fine 102° Fahrenheit mineral waters; so do some of today's visitors. This unspoiled spa also has plenty of seashore.

Since the 16th century, when the village church was built, ARENYS DE MAR has been a seafaring town. Nowadays the fishing fleet is greatly outnumbered by pleasure boats; Arenys's impressive modern marina makes it an international sailing and yachting centre. The town itself climbs from the shore along a stately tree-lined main street. The parish church contains a sumptuous baroque altarpiece which tourists may appreciate better by depositing money in a coin slot to switch on a spotlight.

A good place for camping along the seafront is the busy village of CANET DE MAR. Here you can visit the medieval castle of Santa Florentina.

SANT POL DE MAR, a fishing village with charm, has only about 2,000 inhabitants. Narrow, winding streets lead to an ancient watchtower on top of the promontory. Unlike many a coastal town, it has been able to preserve its character.

CALELLA, also called Calella de la Costa to distinguish it from Calella de Palafrugell (Costa Brava), bustles with tourist development. Eleven-floor blocks of flats and more than 80 hotels house the thousands of visitors who converge here for what the local tourist board calls "cosmopolitan gaiety". Among distinguishing characteristics are a white lighthouse atop a knoll at the south edge of town; an 18th-century church; and a tree-shaded promenade along a very wide sand beach. Its many streets of souvenir shops, bars and restaurants prove Calella's importance as one of the coast's most popular international resorts.

Nearly 2 miles of beaches and unpolluted seawater have made the village of PINEDA DE MAR a delightful tourist attraction.

Next, SANTA SUSANNA is a farming village which has been developed for tourism, with all the modern amenities.

MALGRAT DE MAR is an industrial town of about 10,000. With its 3 miles of beach, it provides the ingredients for a pleasant seaside holiday.

The Costa del Maresme runs out beyond Malgrat. Officially the Costa Brava begins on the other side of the River Tordera. The actual boundary, of scant **19** interest to anyone but a map-maker or tax collector, is a river-bed a couple of hundred yards wide. In summer it's normally bone dry and desolate. In winter, though, water rushes down from the Serra de Montseny in search of the sea. That's when the Tordera turns into a raging flood. It has been known to overflow its banks and even wash away a bridge or two.

Tourists along this stretch of the coast are in a good position to sign up for sea excursions beyond the jurisdictional frontiers. The boats normally call at such celebrated resorts as Blanes, Lloret, Tossa and Sant Feliu de Guíxols. The Costa Brava's spectacular scenery, admired from the sea, justifies its claim to world renown.

Barcelona

Catalonia's capital is a very big city with muscle and brains. Close on two million people live within the boundaries of this centre of banking, publishing and smoky heavy industry. Another million live in the surrounding metropolitan area.

Its main attractions for visitors are renowned—the mighty cathedral, the port, gracious promenades and distinguished museums. You have to be alert for the smaller delights: a noble patio hidden in a slum, a tiled park bench moulded to the anatomy, a street-light fixture lovingly worked in iron, a sculpted gargoyle sneering down from medieval eaves.

The lively people of Barcelona know how to make money. They spend it on flowers and football, music and books, and gooey pastries for their children. They enjoy the bullfights and dancing in the street. They go to gourmet snack-bars

"Aerial ropeway" over Barcelona's port offers panorama of lively city.

and sexy floor-shows, and wear formal evening dress to the opera house.

In the Middle Ages Barcelona was the capital of a surprisingly influential Catalonia. Thirteenth-century Barcelona, ruling distant cities of the Mediterranean, was building big ships in what is today the Maritime Museum, and living by Europe's first code of sea law.

The next great era, economically and artistically, came with late 19th-century industrialization. Politically, the 20th century witnessed a brief revival. In 1931, Barcelona became the capital of an autonomous Catalan Republic, that came to an end in 1939, when the Nationalist forces triumphed. During the Franco era, Catalonia's proud sense of identity was firmly suppressed. But now the language and culture flourish anew, and Barcelona is the hotbed of the region's renaissance.

Gothic Quarter

To walk through 15 centuries of history, through the so-called Gothic Quarter *(Barri Gòtic),* we start, arbitrarily, at the city's present-day hub, the **Plaça de Catalunya** (Catalonia Square). Most of the 21

Estació
Central Sants

C. DE LA INFANTA
CARLOTA JOAQUINA

Carrer de Provença

Carrer de la Creu Coberta

Carrer de Tarragona

Carrer de València

Comte d'Urgell

Roma

Carretera de la Bordeta

Carrer del Consell de Cent

Carrer de Viladomat

Plaça de Toros
Les Arenes

Gran Via de les Corts Catalanes

Plaça
d'Espanya

Gran Via de les Corts Catalanes

Fira Internacional
de Mostres

Carrer de Floridablanca

Comte d'Urgell

Ronda de

Poble Espanyol

Pavelló
Barcelona

Carrer de Lleida

Avinguda del Paral·lel

Carrer de Viladomat

Palau
Nacional

Avinguda de l'Estadi

Museu
Arqueològic

Ronda de Sant Pau

C. de
Sant Pau
del Camp

Fundació
Joan Miró

Avinguda de

Estadi Olímpic

Piscina
Municipal

Carrer Nou de la

Miramar

Passeig de Montjuïc

M o n t

Passeig de Montjuïc

j u ï c

Telefèric

2

Castell de Montjuic

Passeig de Colom

Passeig de Colom

N

BARCELONA

0   250   500 m
0   250   500 yards

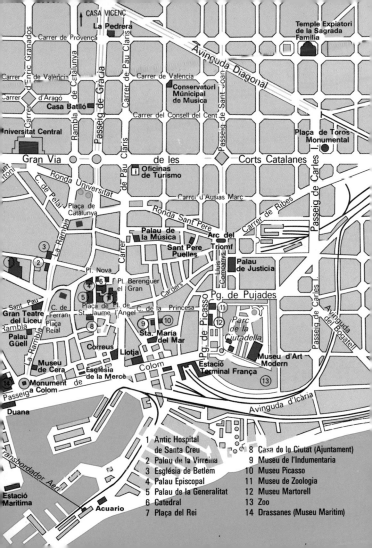

CASA VICENÇ

La Pedrera

Temple Expiatori
de la Sagrada
Familia

Carrer de Provença

Avinguda Diagonal

Carrer de ValèncI

Carrer de València

Carrer de València

Conservatori
Municipal
de Musica

Carrer d'Aragó

Casa Batlló

Carrer del Consell del Cent

Universitat Central

Plaça de Toros
Monumental

Gran Via

de les

Corts Catalanes

Oficinas
de Turisme

Ronda Universitat

C. de Pelai

Carrer d'Ausias Marc

Plaça de
Catalunya

Ronda Sant Pere

Palau de
la Música

Carrer de Ribes

Arc del
Triomf

Sant Pere
Puelles

Pl. Nova

Palau
de Justicia

Gran Teatre
del Liceu

Pl. Berenguer
el Gran

Carders

Pg. de Pujades

Plaça de
St. Jaume l'Àngel

C. de
Ferran

Plaça
Reial

C. de la Princesa

Parc
de la
Ciutadella

Palau
Güell

Correus

Sta. Maria
del Mar

Liotja

Colom

Museu d'Art
Modern

Museu
de Cera

Esglèsia
de la Mercè

Estació
Terminal França

Monument
a Colom

de

la

Mar

Zoo

Passeig a Colom

Avinguda d'Icaria

Duana

Transbordador Aeri

Estació
Maritima

Acuario

1 Antic Hospital
   de Santa Creu
2 Palau de la Virreina
3 Esglèsia de Betlem
4 Palau Episcopal
5 Palau de la Generalitat
6 Catedral
7 Plaça del Rei

8 Casa de la Ciutat (Ajuntament)
9 Museu de l'Indumentaria
10 Museu Picasso
11 Museu de Zoologia
12 Museu Martorell
13 Zoo
14 Drassanes (Museu Maritim)

bus, metro and railway lines converge here.

At the south-eastern edge of the plaza begins a short but important street intriguingly named **Portal de l'Ángel** (Gate of the Angel). As it descends from Plaça de Catalunya, the street narrows; for most hours of the day, it's a pedestrians-only sanctuary, with convenient benches for tired feet.

Gothic Quarter: delights of medieval architecture at every turn.

Avinguda Portal de l'Ángel leads to **Plaça Nova** (New Square), not new at all. In the 13th century, this was a major market area. Now there is an outdoor market on Sundays.

Incongruously, the modern building of the College of Architects overlooks this ancient square. At first glance, you might think the façades of the College had been decorated by children. On second glance, you'd be right in guessing that the author of these huge graffiti could be none other than Pablo Picasso, who contributed these sketches on the theme of Catalan folklore.

From here the spires of the cathedral are already in sight. We'll take a closer look shortly. But first, notice the two stone towers straight ahead. Known as Portal del Bisbe (Bishop's Gate), they were part of the 4th-century Roman wall, raised higher eight centuries later.

Walk between the towers, that is, between the Palau Episcopal (Bishop's Palace), and the Archdeacon's House, and you will immediately feel the other-worldliness of Barcelona's Gothic Quarter. Take a look at the Romanesque patio of the Bishop's Palace, the first of many majestic courtyards to be seen in Barcelona. Very little connection could be claimed between the elegance of these columned precincts and the idea of a Spanish patio of whitewashed stucco.

The patio of the **Casa de l'Ardiaca** (the Archdeacon's House) is more intimate and appealing, with its slim palm tree and moss-covered fountain. The 11th-century building was restored in the early 16th century.

And so to the **Catedral de Santa Eulalia** (St. Eulalia Cathedral), dedicated to a legendary local girl who was tortured and executed for her fervent Christian faith in the 4th century.

The cathedral's construction was begun at the end of the 13th century and lasted for about 150 years. At the end of the 19th century, new work was undertaken thanks to a subsidy from a rich industrialist. Some critics complain that he spoiled the pure Catalan Gothic effect. But don't worry about the critics. Come back one night when the delicate spires are illuminated and light inside glows through the stained-glass windows. It's a pulse-quickening sight by any standards.

The interior of the cathedral is laid out in classic Catalan Gothic form, with three aisles neatly engineered to produce an effect of grandeur and uplift.

Look into the side chapels, with their precious paintings and sculptures. In the chapel of St. Benedict, the lifelike **Altarpiece of the Transfiguration** is the work of a great 15th-century Catalan artist, Bernat Martorell.

The **choir,** in the geometric centre of the cathedral, con-

1 Palau Episcopal
2 Casa de l'Ardiaca
3 Catedral
4 Palau de la Generalitat
5 Casa de la Ciutat (Ajuntament)
6 Saló del Tinell
7 Capella Reial de Santa Agata
8 Museu d'Història de la Ciutat
9 Museu Frederic Marés

centrates dazzling sculptural intricacies. The 15th-century German sculptor Michael Lochner carved the splendid **25** canopies over the choir pews.

A wide stairway leads beneath the high altar to the crypt of the aforementioned St. Eulalia. Notice the rogue's gallery of small stone-carved heads around the stairway and entry arch. The saint's carved alabaster sarcophagus dates from 1327.

For a change to a cheery atmosphere, step into the

cloister, a 15th-century Gothic classic. All cloisters are supposed to be tranquil, and so is this—except for the half dozen argumentative geese who rule the roost here, as have their ancestors for centuries.

The **Museu de la Catedral** (Cathedral Museum) displays religious paintings and sculpture from the 14th century onwards.

Before leaving the cathedral, step into the **Capella de Santa Llucia** (St. Lucy's Chapel), a spartan 13th-century sanctuary built by the bishop whose sepulchre is on view. Notice the 13th- and 14th-century tombstones in the floor. Every step, as they say, touches a bit of history.

Now a few other highlights near the cathedral in the Gothic Quarter:

Museu Frederic Marés. The museum houses an ambitious collection of statues from the 10th century on.

Museu d'Història de la Ciutat (Museum of the History of the City). The average visitor may choose to neglect Barcelona's old maps and documents, collected in this pleasant palace, but the scene below ground is unforgettable. Subterranean passages follow the admirable tracks of Roman civilization. Houses, waterworks, statues and ceramics have been excavated. In search of ballast for the ancient city's defensive towers, they threw in anything at hand including tombs, plaques and upsidedown columns. Now archaeologists are tunnelling under the very cathedral to uncover relics of the Visigoths.

The museum faces Barcelona's most historic square, **Plaça del Rei** (King's Square). According to unconfirmed tradition, Columbus was received on this very spot when he returned a hero from his first voyage to the New World. Ferdinand and Isabella, the Catholic Monarchs, may have sat on the great steps of **Saló del Tinell** (Tinell Hall). They're shown thus, sitting in a famous stylized painting in which American Indians brought back by Columbus fairly swoon with ecstasy at the sight of their new masters.

Whether or not Columbus climbed the ceremonial stairs,

Cathedral tower looms over façade by Picasso. Plaça del Rei (below) is a splendid medieval ensemble.

Tinell Hall would have been a fine spot for his "welcome home" reception. Built in the 14th century, it consists of one immense room with a wood-panelled ceiling supported by six arches. Above the hall is an architectural afterthought of the mid-16th century, the **Torre del Rei Martí** (King Martin's Lookout Tower). This curious accumulation of porti-coed galleries rises five storeys above the hall—just the place to mount a spy-glass to see the sea.

The square is also bounded by the **Capella de Santa Agata** (Chapel of St. Agatha), a 13th-century royal church with a slender tower. The far side of the chapel, facing the modern city, rests on the an-cient Roman wall. You can see it all in detail from the **Plaça de Ramón Berenguer el Gran,** a sort of sunken garden right against the wall.

Plaça Sant Jaume (St. James's Square) lies right in the heart of the city, and in the heart, too, of the Barcelonese, for the square is graced by Barcelona's two most recog-nizable, symbolic buildings: the city hall and the General-itat.

On the north side of the square is the **Palau de la Gene-ralitat,** home of Catalonia's autonomous government. This ceremonious 15th-century structure hides a surprise or two: the overpowering or-namentation of St. George's Room and an upstairs patio with orange trees.

Across the square, the **Casa de la Ciutat** or Ajuntament (city hall) is even older. A sumptuous highlight of this 14th-century political centre is the **Saló del Consell de Cent** (Chamber of the Council of One Hundred), restored to its original glory worthy of any assembly.

But medieval life in Barce-lona was not all pomp and ma-jesty. Just to the west of the Generalitat, narrow streets with names like Call and Ba-nys Nous mark the ancient Jewish Quarter. In the 11th, 12th and 13th centuries, it was a centre of philosophy, poetry and science. The Jews were money-lenders, also, and fi-nanced King Jaime I in his Mediterranean conquests. In 1391, as anti-semitic passions gripped Spain, the Barcelona ghetto was sacked.

La Rambla, relaxed but always dynamic, charms young and old.

La Rambla

Barcelona's best-known promenade, La Rambla, descends gradually but excitingly from Plaça de Catalunya to the port, a distance of about a mile. Like the sun and the shade, the tawdry and shabby share space with the chic and charming all the way down La Rambla. Almost every visitor succumbs to the attraction of this boulevard, thronged day and night with a fascinating crowd of people, animals and things. When you can't walk another inch along the undulating paving designs in the central walkway, watch the parade of the passing crowd from an outdoor café or rent a chair from a concessionaire.

Every couple of cross-streets the Rambla's character subtly changes. So does its official name, five times in all—but that needn't concern us. It may explain why the Rambla is often referred to in the plural as Les Rambles.

The start of the Rambla at the Plaça de Catalunya ought to be its most elegant area, but this is not really so. The air of animation here might baffle or mislead an outsider. Those groups of men spiritedly arguing are not forming political **29**

parties or disputing dogma. They are football fans conducting post-mortems after a match.

Here, too, you can buy a newspaper, magazine or book from the international choice displayed at the news-stands. The Rambla is also the kind of place where you can buy a lottery ticket or one cigarette from a very small businessman.

Not far beyond the Hyde Park Corner of football experts there used to be a university centre. In the 16th and 17th centuries, students congregated here; the name — Rambla dels Estudis — remains.

The huge old **Església de Betlem** (Church of Bethlehem), on the right, looks as if it might be an important attraction. But not in this city of so many truly exceptional churches, big and small.

You can buy a bird or a monkey along here, or just stand and stare at one of many stands dealing in canaries, doves, parrots and pigeons. Beyond the bird zone come the flower kiosks with their year-round colour: local carnations, Canary Islands bird-of-paradise flowers, and potted cacti.

The **Palau de la Virreina** (a reference to the Spanish vice-reine in 18th-century Peru) is one of the most sumptuous buildings on the Rambla. It houses the city hall Department of Culture, as well as the Postal Museum and the Numismatic Cabinet, of great interest to specialists. Other floors of the palace are used for topical exhibitions.

The **Mercat de Sant Josep** (popularly known as *La Boqueria*), one of those classic iron-covered and colonnaded markets of the 19th century, faces the Rambla. You have to wander among the eye-catching displays to appreciate the wealth of fresh fruit and vegetables, meat and seafood available here.

Just behind the market, in the Plaça del Doctor Fleming (honouring the discoverer of penicillin), a profession of bygone centuries endures. In the mornings, four men sit in adjacent small booths, filling the ancient role of scribes. With increasing literacy among the population they now offer a more sophisticated range of services—typing business letters, translating, expediting official forms. But they're still known to ghostwrite a love letter or two. **31**

Travels with Sancho

An early tourist, Don Quixote de la Mancha, had never seen the sea until he visited Barcelona. The most universal fictional hero of all time also toured a publishing house.

In chapter 60 of Book Two of Cervantes' immortal novel, Quixote sums up the rough-tough atmosphere of 16th-century Barcelona, where "they hang outlaws and bandits 20 by 20 and 30 by 30". Running into the macabre aftermath of a mass execution in a forest, Quixote anticipates an old joke and says, "I reckon I must be near Barcelona".

A further detour from the market goes to the **Hospital de la Santa Creu,** now a formidable combination of buildings including the Library of Catalonia and the 18th-century Royal Academy of Medicine and Surgery. See the old operating theatre lit by a great crystal chandelier. A pilgrims' hospital stood here from the beginning of the 13th century.

Back on the Rambla, the main entrance to the **Gran Teatre del Liceu,** the Opera House, almost goes unnoticed. Behind a discreet façade is hidden one of the largest and most majestic auditoriums in the world. (The opera season in Barcelona lasts from December to May.)

Just off the Rambla in Carrer Nou de la Rambla stands one of the grand houses that Gaudí built: Palau Güell. The fortress-

like residence was designed for a Catalan aristocrat (see p. 42).

Carrer Nou de la Rambla and the Rambla itself make up the unofficial boundaries of a district of ill repute called the **Barri Chino** (Chinatown). Prostitution was outlawed in Spain in 1956 but you'd never know it in this part of Barcelona. From midday to dawn the narrow old streets call to mind the darkest corners of Marseilles. You have to be on guard against petty thieves here—bag snatchers in particular.

One more diversion, on the opposite side of the Rambla:

Charming old Spanish-style street transplanted to Poble Espanyol.

the **Plaça Reial** (Royal Square) is Barcelona's most perfectly proportioned square. Try to see it on a Sunday morning, when the stamp- and coin-collectors turn the arcaded square into a market-place. Watch grim-faced professionals, equipped with their own magnifying glasses and tweezers, facing each other across coin trays or stamp albums like so many champion chess players.

Towards the bottom of the promenade you'll find Barcelona's **Museu de Cera** (Wax Museum). In what was once a bank building, the lifelike images of all manner of celebrities are displayed, with special attention to famous murderers.

The Rambla leads on down to the Columbus monument and the port (see p. 37). Whether you stay in the shade of the tall plane trees on the promenade or cross the traffic to window-shop along the edges of the street (where you can buy anything from a guitar to a deep-sea diving-bell), you'll want to walk the Rambla from beginning to end and back again. For better or worse, this is surely where it's all happening.

Montjuïc

It's pronounced mon-ZHWEEK, and whether you reach it by foot, taxi, bus or funicular, you could spend a whole day there and not see everything you ought to.

Montjuïc is a modest mountain less than 700 feet high. Until relatively recently, it had only military significance. But Barcelona's World Exhibition of 1929 saw hundreds of buildings planted upon its hillsides. The best are still there.

The name, Montjuïc, seems to refer to an ancient Jewish cemetery on the site. Or it may be even older, from the Latin Mont Jovis—Jupiter Mountain.

Montjuïc begins, more or less officially, at Plaça d'Espanya, a huge and frightening traffic roundabout. From here, you can look up the hillside, past the commercial exhibition grounds to a great **fountain,** one of Barcelona's prides. On weekend and holiday evenings, the waters are inventively illuminated. The central jet rises as high as 165 feet; water roars up at 642 gallons per second.

Next to the fountain stands the German Pavilion designed by architect Mies van der Rohe for the 1929 Fair and demolished shortly afterwards. Recently reconstructed in a burst of civic pride, it's now known as **El Pavelló Barcelona.**

Looming above all this, with a dome reminiscent of the U.S. Capitol building in Washington, is a palace built as recently as 1929— also for the World Fair. Architecturally, the Palau Nacional won't win any prizes for originality, but it houses the **Museu d'Art de Catalunya** (Museum of Art of Catalonia), one of the world's greatest collections of medieval art. Sixty-eight exhibition halls follow chronological order in this exceptionally well organized museum; but check that it's not closed during extensive renovations.

The 10th- and 11th-century Catalan religious paintings bear a striking resemblance to ancient Byzantine icons. See the beautiful 12th-century wood carvings from church altars, and magnificent frescoes of the same period, rescued from crumbling old churches.

Another leftover from the World Exhibition of 1929, the Palace of Graphic Arts, has been turned into the **Museu Arqueològic** (Archaeological Museum). The prehistoric items come mostly from Catalonia and the Balearic Islands. Many Greek and Roman relics come from Empúries (Ampurias), the Costa Brava town first settled by the Phoenicians in the 6th century B.C. There are also architectural displays from Barcelona's Roman days.

The **Museu Etnològic** (Ethnological Museum) of Montjuïc is devoted to specimens gathered by expeditions to exotic far-off places.

The newest museum on the mountain, opened in 1975, goes under the name of **Fundació Joan Miró.** This complex of original concrete and glass, the work of architect Josep M. Sert, is a tribute to the great Catalan artist Joan Miró, and the intense Catalanism of the place extends to the titles of the works, given in Catalan and occasionally also in French, but never in Spanish. What with the bright architecture and the riot of Miró paintings, sculptures, drawings and tapestries, this is as happy a museum as you're ever likely to see anywhere in the world.

Most conducted tours of Barcelona stop at **Poble Espanyol** ("Spanish Village"), a **35** five-acre exhibition of Spanish art and architecture in the form of an artificial village, which shows the charms and styles of Spain's regions in full scale and super-concentration.

When Don Quixote came to Barcelona, he watched a naval force set out to do battle with pirates thanks to a signal from the lookout point on Montjuïc. This early-warning system by means of flags or bonfires had been operating as early as 1401. But the fortress which stands atop Montjuïc today wasn't built until 1640. It was handed over to the city in 1960 and fitted out as the

La Sagrada Familia: spires of Gaudí church inspire pride in Catalans.

Museu Militar (Military Museum).

From the roof of the fortress, you get a sweeping 360-degree panorama of the metropolis of Barcelona and the sea. You can also look straight down onto the port, with its many fascinations.

For visitors with time to spare, Montjuïc has more attractions in reserve—a Greek amphitheatre, sports installations, meticulously landscaped terraced gardens, and an amusement park with the full complement of roller-coaster, Ferris wheel and other thrilling rides, plus a special children's amusement park.

The Waterfront *

The boosters of Barcelona always seem to be searching for superlatives. They call this the biggest city on the Mediterranean shore. They also claim that the **Monument a Colom** (Columbus Monument), between the port and the Rambla, is said to be the tallest monument to Columbus in the world. There is a lift inside

_____
* The only thing the next items have in common is the geographical coincidence that they are on or near the Barcelona waterfront. They cover a wide swath of the city and a broad range of interests—perhaps something for everybody.

the column, which takes you to the upper platform, from where there is an extraordinary view out over Barcelona and the sea.

Glass-and-steel commercial buildings may come and go, but the **Reials Drassanes,** or medieval shipyards, are most special. The first work on what became this sprawling construction began in the 13th century. This is the only structure of its kind in the world today—an impressive testimony to the level of Catalan industrial architecture in the Middle Ages.

From these royal dockyards were launched the ships which carried the red-and-yellow Catalan flag to the far corners of the world as it was known before Columbus. Since 1941 the **Museu Marítim** (Maritime Museum) has occupied these appropriate quarters.

The most engrossing display is a full-sized reproduction of the galley *Real*, victorious flagship in the Battle of Lepanto of 1571, where a combined Hispano-Venetian fleet faced the Turks. Elsewhere you can inspect models of fishing boats and freighters, and glamorous ship figureheads. In the cartography department, look for an **37** atlas drawn in 1439, which once belonged to Amerigo Vespucci.

Across an extremely wide and heavily congested thoroughfare, an unexpected annexe of the Maritime Museum is moored at the wharf of Portal de la Pau (Gate of Peace). This is a replica of the *Santa María,* Columbus's own flagship—full-sized and said to

Sightseeing tours of Barcelona's busy port include cooling breezes.

be authentically fitted out. You may board the floating minimuseum any time during the day.

Like all big ports, this area of Barcelona is strong on atmosphere. Longshoremen rub shoulders with amateur rod-and-reel-fishermen; guitar-

strumming tourists lie back on their knapsacks waiting for the ferryboat to Ibiza. Tugs nudge a huge white cruise liner to a soft berthing. Sightseeing boats, romantically called *golondrinas* (swallows), stand by to show tourists the harbour from sea-level.

From Plaça Portal de la Pau the boulevard of **Moll de Bosch i Alsina** provides a charming promenade by the sea.

A largely artificial peninsula protecting the port area from the open sea is called **La Barceloneta** (Little Barcelona). The residents are something like the local equivalent of Cockneys—certainly "characters" different from the rest. Barcelona's most popular seafood restaurants are found in this old fishermen's district. As an 18th-century experiment in urban planning, Barceloneta's street plan is worth a closer look. The blocks are long and uncommonly narrow so that each room of each house faces a street.

Several bus lines terminate at the Passeig Nacional, Barceloneta, site of the city's **Aquari** (Aquarium). Unlike the fishy section of the Barcelona Zoo (see p. 45), this aquarium con-

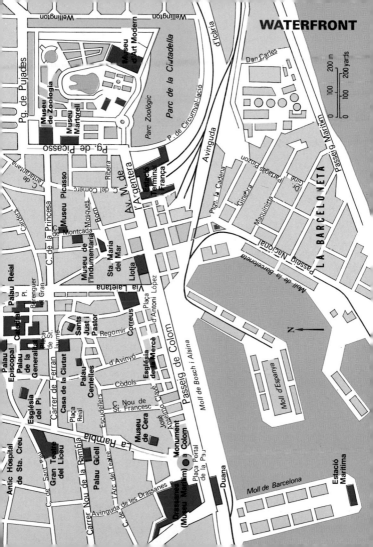

cerns itself only with the sea life of the Mediterranean. The lighting is gloomy—for the benefit of the fish, not the people.

Railway yards separate Barceloneta from the Parc de la Ciutadella (see p. 44). The terminal is called Estació de França because trains from France arrive here.

La Llotja is the Barcelona stock exchange. Since the 14th century, a *bolsa* (exchange) of one sort or another has oper-
40 ated on this spot.

The cornerstone of the **Església de Santa Maria del Mar** (Church of St. Mary-of-the-Sea) was laid in 1329. More than any other edifice in Barcelona, this one sums up the real grandeur of 14th-century Catalan churches. The stark beauty of the interior is heightened by the proportions of its soaring arches. The impression of immensity comes, in part, from the uncluttered lines. In addition to its religious functions, Santa Maria del Mar is often used as a concert hall for programmes of classical music or jazz. It faces the site of medieval tournaments, carnivals processions... and the executions of the Inquisition.

Carrer de Montcada just beyond would make a worthwhile visit even if it didn't contain one of Barcelona's most popular museums. As early as the 12th century, noble families of Catalonia had begun to build their mansions in this street. You can see their crests carved in stone alongside great portals. Better still, wander into the courtyards of the palaces and relive the glory of those medieval achievements.

The **Museu Picasso** is located in three contiguous 13th-century palaces in Carrer de

Montcada. Though Pablo Ruiz Picasso was born in Málaga, he came to Barcelona at the age of 14 to study art. Those days are documented by drawings and paintings in a style evidently imposed on the young genius by unimaginative teachers. But his true talents, from an even earlier age, are strikingly clear in informal sketches, cartoons and doodles. His large oil painting *Science and Charity,* could have been the work of a master; he was 15 at the time. One large exhibition is devoted to a series of 58 paintings which Picasso donated to the museum in 1968. Of these, 44 are bizarre variations on the theme of *Las Meninas,* the famous Velázquez painting in Madrid's Prado Museum.

An important collection of prints—over 100 artist's proofs spanning the decades from the 1920s through the '60s—has gone on view.

Across the street, in another lovely palace, the city of Barcelona has opened the **Museu de l'Indumentaria** (Costume Museum). Fashions for men, women and children as far back as the 16th century are exhibited according to period and use.

Spain's best-known modern sculptor, Antoni Tapiès, pays homage to Picasso in an eccentric fountain sculpture installed on the nearby Passeig de Picasso. Water gushes in and around a glass cube enclosing some old chairs and a sofa—bound with rope, bristling with steel beams and draped with a cloth. Picasso would have been amused.

Gaudí and "Eixample"

"Eixample" means extension or enlargement. In Barcelona, it means the new city which grew beyond the medieval walls in the 19th century. The expansion, several times the area of the existing city, was well planned. Its fine boulevards— the Passeig de Gràcia and Rambla de Catalunya, for instance—are expressions of elegance. The very long, wide **Avinguda Diagonal** is not only the main traffic artery from the motorway (expressway) into the city, but an eminently stately avenue with palm trees and interesting architecture.

The "Eixample" contains some of the most creative buildings ever designed, the work of Barcelona's inspired *art nouveau* architects at the **41** end of the 19th and beginning of the 20th centuries. The greatest of them all was Antoni Gaudí, a controversial genius born in the Catalonian market town of Reus in 1852. He died in Barcelona in 1926, run down by a tram.

Here are half a dozen typical Gaudí projects you could see in one outing, starting in Old Barcelona and working your way out through the "Eixample":

The **Palau Güell,** one of several buildings Gaudí designed for his friend and patron, Eusebio Güell, a British-educated Barcelona industrialist, civic leader and nobleman. This palace, just off the bustling Rambla (see p. 33), keeps its biggest innovations out of public view: its front façade, decorated with imaginative ironwork, lacks Gaudí's wit and colour. The rooftop chimney array is so original that it relieves some of the severity.

Casa Batlló. People emerging from the Metro (underground railway) here in Passeig de Gràcia may be startled to come face to face with Gaudí's sensuous curves in stone and iron, and his delicate tiles. The house next door, the Casa Amatller by the brilliant Cata-

lan architect Puig i Cadafalch, conflicts with Gaudí's effort so aggressively that this group of houses is often called the Block of Discord (in Spanish, this involves an ironic play on words).

Casa Milá ("La Pedrera").

One of Gaudí's classic buildings: Casa Batlló, in Passeig de Gràcia.

On the corner of Passeig de Gràcia and Carrer de Provença, this big block of flats stirs strong feelings. Some say it's too heavy, a stone monstrosity; Gaudí fans love its undulating façade, adorned with original wrought-iron-work, and the famous roof-terrace with its weird formations covering chimneys and ventilators.

Casa Vicenç. This was designed more than 20 years earlier than Casa Milá, when Gaudí was still groping for his style. In fact, Casa Vicenç, a summer home for a rich tile merchant, was Gaudí's first big job as an architect. The distinctive ironwork, the bright ideas with tile may rate admiration, but the overall effect seems incoherent.

Parc Güell. This incomparably inventive park started out as a suburban real estate development which failed. Count Güell and Gaudí wanted to create a perfect garden city for 60 families. But only two houses were sold (Gaudí bought one of them). The happy originality of Güell Park, bought by the city of Barcelona in 1926, delights young and old. See the ginger-bread-type houses, the cheery use of tiles, the huge serpentine bench bordering the main plaza. Explore the grounds and discover that the plaza is in fact the roof for what would have been a market-place supported by a thicket of 96 mock-classical columns. The last column in each regiment is playfully askew. Along the woods, walk under the perilously tilted arcade.

Temple Expiatori de la Sagrada Familia (Holy Family). Gaudí's eternally unfinished "sandcastle cathedral" must be seen; you may not believe it. Wild and wonderful, it is an extravagant hymn to one man's talent and faith. In his first four towers, was Gaudí consciously or unconsciously echoing the filigree of the classic cathedral in the Gothic Quarter? Or the shape of "human castles" of Catalan folk-lore? If he had lived, would he have continued in the same way? Can one building, however immense, ever successfully combine so many disparate styles? Gaudí's cathedral produces puzzlement and awe. Many Catalans see this stupendous church as an extension of their own faith and strivings; their donations keep the construction work going. **43**

Don't be afraid of the huge cranes hauling pillars and streamlined arches into position. Where else can you stand inside a roofless cathedral and watch it being built? Before your eyes descendants of the great Catalan stonecutters are shaping the faces of angels.

Ciutadella

The residents of Barcelona greatly appreciate the Parc de la Ciutadella (Park of the Citadel) because it is a big, green refuge from the congestion of the city. They also appreciate it for symbolic reasons going back to the early 18th century.

In those days, the area, called La Ribera, was a pleasant residential suburb of perhaps 10,000 people. Because Barcelona fought on the losing side in the War of the Succession, a vengeful Philip V ordered Ribera levelled. Then he conscripted all the carpenters and masons of Barcelona to build a fortress on the spot.

In the middle of the 19th century, this building of bitter memories was at last demolished. And, characteristically, in its place, the city built a park with gardens, lakes and promenades.

The great fountain is one of those monumental excesses typical of the period. This titanic mass of sculpture looks like a work of a committee, and indeed it was. One of the contributors was Gaudí, then a student of architecture.

The **Museu d'Art Modern** is actually devoted to Catalan

Beloved Barcelona fountain keeps statue of lady dry under umbrella.

art of the last 100 years. Outstanding here are the works of such great painters as Isidre Nonell, Ramon Casas and Mariano Fortuny, the latter a native of Reus, Gaudí's home town near Tarragona. Notice the wealth of astutely recorded detail in *The Vicarage,* and you can't miss *The Battle of Tetuán,* an action-packed panorama which fills a whole wall. Fortuny knew whereof he painted; he was the 19th-century equivalent of a combat photographer in Morocco.

Looking Down

Barcelona is crazy about views from on high.

A modern, modified cable-car built with Swiss technical assistance, floats high above the city between the Estació Funicular and Montjuïc. An elaborate "aerial ropeway" *(transbordador)* strung from towers 426 feet high serves a similar purpose between the port and Montjuïc.

If you have a queasy stomach, try the less daring cog railway running up to Tibidabo.

For a superb panorama of Barcelona, go up to the fortress high on the summit of Montjuïc (see pp. 36–37 or to the temple of Tibidabo (p. 46).

If time's short, ascend the pillar supporting the Columbus Statue in the port.

Upstairs the museum shows a hotch-potch of modern art, sculpture and *art-nouveau* furnishings.

A sizeable corner of the park is devoted to the **Barcelona Zoo,** an admirable modern version of the conventional collection of animals. Under a reform programme of the 1950s the zoo eliminated fences, using instead moats or

Star of the show at Barcelona zoo: albino gorilla thrives in captivity.

lakes to separate the public from the fauna. Young and old can enjoy six well planned departments: African animals, felines, monkeys, reptiles, birds and fish. A great attraction of the zoo, especially for children, are the dolphin and the killerwhale shows. **45**

Pedralbes

Barcelona's richest residential area, Pedralbes, consists of fashionable blocks of flats, earlier *art nouveau* buildings, and villas discreetly guarded by ornamental fences. (One of those fences—by Gaudí—in Avinguda Pedralbes, is a first-class work of art in itself.)

The **Palau de Pedralbes,** set in a charming park, looks quite livable. The palace was built in the 1920s as a municipal gift to King Alfonso XII. Most of the furnishings and works of art were imported from Italy. The king didn't get to enjoy it much, as he was forced to abdicate in 1931.

The palace houses a charming museum of carriages and the **Colecció Cambó,** a magnificent collection of paintings by the greatest Italian, French, Spanish and Dutch artists, assembled by a Catalan named Francesc Cambó.

The other important sight of Pedralbes, one of Barcelona's finest historic buildings, is the **Monestir de Pedralbes.** It was founded in 1326 by Elisenda de Montcada, the queen of Jaime II; she is buried in the monastery's Catalan Gothic church. Several dozen nuns live here today.

The cloister, with 25 arches on each side, rises three storeys high. You can meditate (briefly) among the poplars and orange trees in the quadrangle. But don't miss the monastery's greatest artistic treasure, in a cramped little chapel lit by two fluorescent tubes. The murals here were painted by Ferrer Bassa, the greatest 14th-century Catalan artist.

Tibidabo

For a first, or last, look at Barcelona no place excels Tibidabo, a mountain about 1,650 feet above the city. On an average of once a month, when visibility is flawless, it's said you can see the mountains of Majorca from here. On an ordinary day you can look down on all Barcelona and a slice of the Costa Dorada as well. Tibidabo can be reached by car, or by an adventurous combination of train, tram and cable car. It's a very popular excursion for the people of Barcelona, especially on a Sunday.

The shrine at the summit is the Templo Expiatorio del Sagrado Corazón (Expiatory Temple of the Sacred Heart of Jesus), a neo-Gothic extravaganza erected in 1911. A huge statue of a Christ with outstretched arms stands upon the topmost tower.

Just beneath the church is a big amusement park with a roller coaster, an old-fashioned aeroplane-go-round, and other rides for children or light-hearted adults. The **Museu d'Autòmats** (Mechanical Dolls Museum) contains one of the most enchanting collections of those 19th-century toys. There are also hotels on Tibidabo, as well as restaurants, snack-bars, sports facilities, an observatory and a TV tower.

Nothing shy about the pigeons in Plaça de Catalunya at lunch time.

Sitges and the Coast South of Barcelona

The coastal landscape on the south side of Barcelona has its share of cliffs and coves, but consists mainly of broad sand beaches. For variety there are appealing fishing villages, and even a stretch of green paddy fields. Along with the scenery and water sports the region is rich in history and culture.

Leaving Barcelona towards the south-west the suburbs can't seem to decide whether they are agricultural or factory towns—or just half-hearted resorts. Whatever the label, the near outskirts hold practically no interest for tourists. (A vital exception is the international airport, close by the sea at El Prat de Llobregat.)

The first resort town following El Prat, CASTELLDEFELS, enjoys an extremely long sand beach. Low-rise hotels, apartment houses and villas exploit the coastline, while the town centre looks inland. In the 13th century, when Castelldefels first entered the history books, the sea was a danger. Watch-towers, some still standing, guarded against pirates. The castle which gave the town its name, impressive enough from afar, has become dilapidated since

its last renovation in 1897.

A small **museum** is maintained in a restored mansion below the castle. The exhibits in the Casa de Cultura include prehistoric tools and 19th-century farm implements.

Beyond Castelldefels the railway line cuts through mountains, while the road winds around them the hard way, often skirting cliffsides dramatically. Two villages appear at unexpected inlets. GARRAF, an industrial town, has a marina and unobtrusive villas. VALLCARCA, with its own cargo port, is not a tourist town at all.

By the time the coastline begins to level out, the scene changes dramatically. **Sitges,** an internationally admired resort, combines natural beauty, liveliness and dignity.

Sitges is one of the rare Spanish coastal resorts which has maintained its identity, avoiding the monstrosities of tourist architecture while still encouraging tourism. This is one town without repetitive high-rise hotels. The swinging "downtown" area lives one life; further along the seafront promenade, the "other half"— largely wealthy families from Barcelona—enjoys a quieter

existence in villas hidden behind high, trimmed hedges. The beach is nearly three miles long—enough for crowd-lovers and seekers of serenity as well. Bathing is safe for children, as it tends to be all the way from here to Tarragona and beyond.

The parish church, on a promontory, was built between the 16th and 18th centuries,

Surfboard plus sail equals exciting sport, only for the well-balanced.

but sacked during the Civil War. It may not be an architectural gem, but its dramatic setting makes up for that; at night, it is skilfully illuminated **49** against the sky. Just behind the church, two museums contribute to the cultural atmosphere which helps explain the town's long-standing appeal to artists and intellectuals. The **Museu Cau Ferrat** (Cau Ferrat—or "iron lair"—Museum) contains a moving El Greco portrait, *The Tears of St. Peter*, as well as a blazingly colourful early oil by Picasso, *Corrida de toros*. Here you can also see many works by Santiago Rusiñol (1861–1931), the Catalan artist and writer who gave the building to the town. Next-door, the **Museu Mar i Cel** (Sea and Sky Museum), in a 14th-century palace, displays medieval sculpture and religious paintings. A few streets inland, another museum is aimed at people who don't normally go to museums, least of all at a resort. The **Museu Romàntic** (Romantic Museum) of Sitges is an old aristocratic home lavishly decorated in 19th-century style and full of the fascinating *things* of the era—furniture, clocks and music boxes that work.

With its whitewashed houses facing narrow hilly streets, its gourmet restaurants, pizza parlours and flamenco nightclubs, and its mild climate, Sitges attracts holiday-makers over many months of the year. A very special time, however, comes every spring. At the fiesta of Corpus Christi the streets are covered with fresh flowers—a quarter of a million of them, in inventive patterns. The beauty couldn't be more fleeting, for the flower carpets last just one day.

A few miles down the coast

After an exhausting day of tanning, tourists stroll beneath the palms of Sitges and plan the night's agenda.

50

the city of VILANOVA I LA GELTRÚ has an extensive sand beach but much less tourist development than Sitges.

Befitting a town of about 45,000 people, there is a serious museum—the **Museu Balaguer** —devoted mainly to 19th-century paintings by Catalan artists.

Vilanova i la Geltrú also has its non-serious museum, a first cousin of the Romantic Museum in Sitges. **Casa Papiol,** an 18th-century mansion, re-creates a vanished way of life— right down to the stables and wine-cellar, and a trim garden in which swans reside alongside magnificent peacocks.

The only excitements between the villages of CUBELLES and CUNIT are the River Foix and the boundary line dividing the provinces of Barcelona and Tarragona.

Slightly further down the coast, CALAFELL is much more of a tourist centre. With its two-mile long beach, Calafell was a natural choice for exploitation.

Shortly inland from Calafell lies EL VENDRELL, an important wine town and shopping centre and the birthplace of cellist Pablo Casals (1876–1973).

COMARRUGA, with nearly three miles of sand beach, has been transformed into a fashionable holiday resort with big hotels to supplement its comfortable villas. It's a spa and sporting centre as well.

The coast road along here— usually jammed in summer— follows the Roman highway to Tarragona. A startling reminder of this confronts motorists not far beyond Comarruga. In the middle of the road stands a triumphal arch—not one of those ugly neo-classical models commemorating some recent war, but the real thing. This well-proportioned monument, tall as a three-floor building has been there since the 2nd century A.D. The **Arc de Berà** (Arch of Berà), as it's called, now stands in a position of honour in a small island of green; instead of going under the arch, as it did for hundreds of years, the road now makes a detour around it.

TORREDEMBARRA, the next big resort centre, is expanding along its wide sand beach with new hotels, villas and flats. The local castle, until recently in private hands is restored by the government.

The next castle down the road, in the inland town of **51**

ALTAFULLA, is said to have been begun in the 11th century. Altafulla is the kind of village where the children wave at foreigners. Its medieval back streets are as quiet as a museum.

TAMARIT Castle, visible from afar, juts out above the sea. Even though holiday-makers swim from beaches on either side of Tamarit, the castle looks thoroughly invulnerable. It may have been built in the 11th century, but has been considerably restored since then.

Finally, three notable historical sites as the traveller approaches the Tarragona area.

El Medol, a Roman stone-quarry, is right along the motorway *(autopista)* at the last service area before Tarragona. This man-made crater provided some of the stone for the Roman developments in Tarragona. You can almost see the same grain in the rock as in the great blocks of the city wall.

Right at the edge of the old coast road (N.340), the so-called **Torre de los Escipiones** (Tower of the Scipios) was a Roman funeral monument. Little can be said with assurance about this structure, probably a 1st century A.D. tomb. The sculpted figures of two men in Roman military dress can still be distinguished, but time has erased most other details.

The considerate highway engineers provided parking space and sightseeing facilities in honour of another ancient structure along the route,

Seaside apparition near Tarragona: austere, daunting Tamarit Castle.

known locally as **Pont del Diable** (Devil's Bridge). This perfect Roman aqueduct, a double-decker of stone, carried Tarragona's water supply from the River Gayá. No viaduct of today is more sound or practical—or more graceful.

Tarragona

Pop. 120,000
(Barcelona, 98 km.)

In the 3rd century B.C., the Romans landed at Tarragona and set up military and political headquarters. They liked its strategic location, mild climate and wine. So will you.

Tarraco, as the town was called, became the capital of

Rome's biggest Spanish province. It grew to a population of 30,000 and coined its own money. It was one of the formidable imperial capitals of Antiquity. So much was built, and so much remains, that Tarragona sometimes feels like a time machine. Turn a corner and you flip from the 20th century to the 15th, or the 1st.

For example: **Plaça de la Font,** an apparently unexceptional spot to begin a walking tour of Tarragona. The middle of this elongated oblong plaza is now a municipal car park. The city hall occupies one end. But Plaça de la Font is built on the site of the Roman Circus, the 2nd or 3rd century A.D. precursor of a bullring.

Just behind the city hall, a modern avenue called Vía de l'Imperi skilfully recreates the grace of Roman times. The

Romans constructed amphitheatre overlooking the sea in Tarragona.

mosaics are reminiscent of the walks of Pompeii. The Roman column is authentic. This short street climbs to one of Tarragona's outstanding features: the **Passeig Arqueològic** (archaeological promenade), a close-up tour of the ancient city wall.

Nothing here is more than **53**

about 2,100 years old—even the foundation of the wall, composed of titanic uncut stones weighing up to 35 tons each. They are often referred to as "cyclopean" because of their enormity and irregular shape.

Not only is the wall, with its towers and gateways, a notable historical and architectural attraction, there are also fine panoramas of the countryside and the sea. But don't be misled when you discover, just down the hill, a well preserved open-air Greek theatre. It's a municipal auditorium, built in 1970.

The Passeig Arqueològic, among other impressive ancient sites in Tarragona, is revealed in all its glory on summer nights, when it's bathed in illumination.

Leaving the last gateway, we follow the Passeig Torroja outside the wall as it curves toward the sea. A small park surrounding the Creu de Sant Antoni (St. Anthony's Cross) erected in 1604 faces one of the main gates of the walled city. The Portal de Sant Antoni (St. Anthony's Gateway) leads into the labyrinth of medieval Tarragona, a markedly Mediterranean city with flowerpots in the windows, laundry hanging out to dry and canaries in cages on the walls.

If you can resist wandering at random through this splash of local colour, stick to the Vía Granada until you reach the Plaça del Rei (King's Square). The **Museu Arqueològic** here is a modern, well designed exhibit of delicate mosaics, ancient utensils, pre-Roman, Roman and Spanish coins.

Adjoining the museum, the building once known as the King's Castle is now called the **Pretori Romà** (Roman Pretorium). This much-restored 2,000-year-old fortress contains more archaeological items, including a beautifully sculpted marble sarcophagus found in the sea. You can follow underground passages which linked the castle with the circus (now Plaça de la Font). The vaults served as dungeons in Antiquity, and again during the Spanish Civil War.

Walking from here toward the sea, you can look down upon the Roman **amphitheatre** built into the hillside. During excavations in 1953, an early Christian church was found on the site of the amphitheatre. Presumably, the primitive basilica was a memorial to a bish-

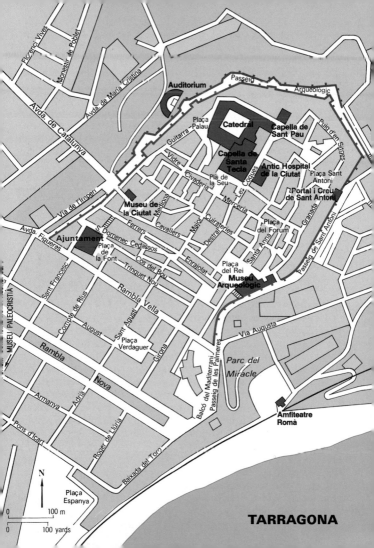

Florenci Vives
Monestir de Poblet
Avda. de María Cristina
Avda. de Catalunya
Auditorium
Passeig
Arqueologic
Plaça
Palau
Catedral
Capella de
Sant Pau
Puig d'en Sitges
Guitarra
Vidre
Capella de
Santa
Tecla
Civaderia
Pla de
la Seu
Antic Hospital
de la Ciutat
Coques
Plaça Sant
Antoni
Via de Hippen
Museu de
la Ciutat
Mediona
Merceria
Portal i Creu
de Sant Antoni
Avda. Figueres
Ajuntament
St. Domenec
Ferrers
Cedassos
Cavallers
Major
Cuiràteries
Destre
Plaça
del Forum
Passeig de Sant Antoni
Granada
Plaça
de la Font
Cos del Bou
Enrajolat
Santa Anna
MUSEU PALEOCRISTIÀ
Sant Francesc
Comte de Rius
Trinquet Nou
Plaça
del Rei
Museu
Arqueologic
Rambla Vella
August
Sant Agustí
Girona
Via Augusta
Plaça
Verdaguer
Rambla
Parc del
Miracle
Nova
Armanya
Adrià
Roser de Lúria
Balcó del Mediterrani /
Passeig de les Palmeres
Amfiteatre
Romà
Pons d'Icart
Baixada del Toro
N
Plaça
Espanya
0   100 m
0   100 yards

TARRAGONA

op and two deacons burned to death there in A.D. 259.

Here, above the ruins and the sea, begins what's called the **Balcó del Maditerrani** (Balcony of the Mediterranean), a cliffside promenade, Tarragona's pride. The view of the sea is unbeatable.

Tarragona's **Rambla** runs uphill and ends at the Balcony of the Mediterranean. Otherwise, it's reminiscent of Barcelona's famous promenade, with many trees, outdoor cafés and a great variety of shops all along it. The statue at the top end of the Rambla honours Admiral Roger de Lauria, a swashbuckling 13th-century hero of the Kingdom of Catalonia and Aragon.

Two other important ancient sites—beyond the area of the walking tour—must be mentioned before we turn to medieval Tarragona.

Near the central market and post office, with its entrance in Carrer Lleida, the remains of the **Roman Forum** have been unearthed. Unlike most archaeological excavations, this one is *above* the level of the present-day city, so two halves of the forum are now connected by a footbridge above Carrer Soler. You can

wander around the area at will, visualizing the layout of houses, shops and other amenities. This well-kept open-air museum is completely hemmed in by a modern city, yet keeps a stately calm.

On the edge of the city, overlooking the River Francolí, an extraordinary museum has been established in an unlikely place. The **Necròpoli i Museu**

Paleocristià (Necropolis and Paleo-Christian Museum), a cemetery for Tarragona's early Christians, is about as big as three football fields. The site has been left essentially as it was. You can walk along the observation platforms looking down upon hundreds of graves, urns and even bones lying where they were uncovered. And in the adjoining museum you can see the best of the finds. Several 5th-century sarcophagi are sculpted with astounding skill.

Medieval Tarragona

Walking up Carrer Sant Agustí from the Rambla, the old city soon closes in. By the time the street's name has changed—to Major—you can feel the throb of real mainstream Mediterranean life. The road turns a bend and suddenly the **Cathedral** comes into view, strangely cropped at the edges by its elevation and the narrowness of the street.

A flight of 19 steps leads from the end of Carrer Major to the Plà de la Seu, an attractive, almost intimate square before the church. But don't overlook the last cross-

street before the cathedral—the Mercería (Haberdashery Street) with its medieval porticoes. A shop here advertises canaries; a female costs half the price of a male (presumably because females can't sing).

Ancient tomb sculpture (opposite) is one facet of Tarragona beauty. Streets, cathedral add to mood.

Surrounding walls and tricks of perspective may distort your estimation of the cathedral's size. The area of the façade is deceptive. But the great Gothic doorway, and one of Europe's largest rose windows above it, provide a clue.

Follow the arrows to the tourist entrance, far around the church to the left, via the cloister. Construction of this cathedral, on the site of a Roman temple to Jupiter, was begun in 1171, and it was consecrated in 1331. The architectural styles inside the cathedral mix Romanesque and Gothic; the overall effect, looking up at the great vaulted ceiling, is austere majesty.

The **main altarpiece,** carved in alabaster by the 15th-century Catalan master Pere Johan, shows splendid lifelike detail. It is dedicated to St. Thecla, the local patron saint. She is said to have been converted to Christianity by St. Paul, who, according to legend, preached in Tarragona.

To the right of the high altar is the tomb of Prince Don Juan de Aragón, an archbishop of Tarragona who died in 1334 at the age of 33. Note the sensitive carving on the sepulchre. The artist's identity is un-

known; the influence seems to be Italian.

Nineteen chapels fill the sides of the church. Their design and decoration tend to extremes—either unforgettably beautiful, or unexpectedly 19th-century kitsch. Don't miss **three chapels:** Capella de Nostra Senyora de Montserrat (Chapel of Our Lady of Montserrat), with its 15th-century altarpiece; the filigreed sculpture in the 14th-century Capella de Santa Maria dels Sastres (Chapel of St. Mary of the Tailors) and the 18th-century Capella de Santa Tecla (Chapel of St. Thecla).

And if the art appreciation and sheer foot-slogging become a bit too much, just take a seat in the congregation and look up at the sunbeams piercing the filters of the rose window.

Outside, again, the **cloister** offers some surprises. First, its size—some 150 feet down each side. The quadrangle is so big that there is little shade, and perhaps less feeling of serenity than in other cloisters of the 12th and 13th centuries. But notice the sculptural innovations and details. Everyone stops to figure out the relief known as the Procession of the

Rats, a wry fable carved 700 years before the invention of Mickey Mouse. Built into one of the walls is another unexpected feature—a Moslem monument of marble. The date on its inscription works out to A.D. 960. This *mihrab* or shrine is believed to have arrived in Tarragona as a battle trophy.

The cathedral's **Museu Dio-**

Fishermen back from sea assign repair of nets to their womenfolk.

cesà (Diocesan Museum) possesses prehistoric and Roman archaeological relics, medieval religious paintings, and a large and valuable collection of tapestries.

Tarragona-on-Sea

For a drastic change of pace, take a bus or taxi, or a very long walk, down to the Tarragona waterfront district unaccountably known as **El Serrall** (the harem). This is clearly an important fishing centre, a radical escalation from the usual quaint port found elsewhere along this coast. In the afternoon the big trawlers come back from the open sea. Trays of ice and big refrigerated lorries are waiting on the quayside. Before disembarking, the tanned fishermen clean and separate the different species of fish in the hold. They swallow the last trickle of wine from the ship's *porrón,* then step ashore to bargain with wholesalers over prices. Elsewhere along the quay, half a dozen women seated under parasols mend the huge fishnets bound for sea before the next dawn.

For local colour, and aroma, El Serrall is hard to match. If you have half a chance, eat in one of the nearby fish restaurants. Tarragona cooking is known far and wide in Catalonia, and the ingredients couldn't be fresher.

South-West of Tarragona

While Tarragona has its own municipal beaches, the nearest resort of international renown is **Salou,** about 10 kilometres down the coast. This cosmopolitan centre calls itself Playa de Europa (beach of Europe). Salou's good fortune is due to its two-mile-long beach, bor-

The town of Salou (pronounced Sal-OH-oo) distinguishes itself with almost universal good taste: the villas and blocks of flats maintain high architectural standards, the gardens are well kept and even the modern monument to James I the Conqueror fits right into place. The beach at Salou was the port of embarcation for James' armada which

dered by a lavish promenade with solid rows of stubby palm trees and masses of colourfully arranged flowers. What's more, swimmers who need more adventure can desert the beach and opt for half-hidden coves around rugged Cape Salou.

60

Real life along the coast: fishermen crouch over nets, while shoppers exchange strong opinions.

wrested Majorca from the Moors in 1229.

Salou's suburb of VILAFORTUNY, with another long beach, consists primarily of exclusive villas protected by high fences or hedges. The landscaping is exceptional.

CAMBRILS, often described as a "typical seafaring village", is a standard fishing port which happens to interrupt the solid line of beaches down the coast. Its charm centres on the large fleet of *bous*—small fishing boats carrying over-sized lamps for night duty. Cambrils can claim to be something of a gourmet town. Its waterfront counts more fine seafood restaurants than many a metropolis. Enthusiasts drive there from miles around, not for the water sports nor the scenery, but just for a meal.

MIAMI PLATJA has plenty of sand and sea, yet doesn't quite live up to the glamour of its name. It's just a quiet resort community of villas and apartments and family hotels. But the setting is dramatic—hills and cliffs push right onto the beaches.

The small resort of L'HOSPITALET DE L'INFANT (Hospice of the Prince) is built alongside the ruins of a 14th-century

hospice for pilgrims, after which the town was named.

Between L'Hospitalet and the next resort on the coast, L'Ametlla de Mar, the shore is almost undeveloped, with one startling exception. The nuclear power station of Vandellós looms up like a science-fiction spaceport. At any rate, the titanic red and white main building looks as if it would be

more comfortable at Cape Canaveral than on this beachfront. Power lines fan out into the countryside.

L'AMETLLA, by happy contrast, is a no-nonsense, picture-postcard fishing village. Four nearby beaches make it some- **61** thing of a tourist centre, but this hasn't marred the town's picturesque charm. With its solid sea-wall, Fishermen's Guild, ice factory and a few cafés, it remains a genuine fishing port.

Just past the small port of L'AMPOLLA, the remarkable **Ebro Delta** begins. This lush, tropical peninsula — more than 100 square miles — was created from the mud travelling down the River Ebro all the way from Zaragoza. The river continues its land reclamation work and the delta expands quite perceptibly each year. A rich rice-growing district, it's all so flat that sometimes, with the reeds growing tall along the back roads, the level of the canals seems higher than the road. The delta is a rallying point for migratory birds — and for bird-watchers with binoculars or cameras.

AMPOSTA, a town of nearly 15,000 people, dominates the delta. It is considered a key centre for sports fishing. In earlier times, Amposta guarded the river route and charged a toll on ships heading inland.

TORTOSA (population 50,000) commands both banks of the Ebro, which explains its strategic importance since ancient times. Julius Caesar awarded Tortosa the title of independent municipality. The elaborate fortress at the top of the town belonged to the Moors, who held out there at length during the Christian Reconquest in 1148. The castle of San Juan is still known by its Arabic name, La Zuda.

Tortosa's **cathedral,** now a national monument, appears at first sight to be abandoned and menaced by the town around it. But you can enter through the cloister, which is well shaded by tall pines. The cathedral, built during the 14th, 15th and 16th centuries, is a classic example of Catalan Gothic. Don't miss the 14th-century triptych, painted on wood, and the two 15th-century carved stone pulpits.

Attempts to make the River Ebro a major navigational channel—Aragon's age-old dream of an outlet to the sea— have been dormant for 50 years. But the river still permeates everyday life in Tortosa. It looks as if it's carrying all the soil of Spain out to the Mediterranean—not the sort of river you'd want to swim in.

The last town of any note along the coast, before the provincial boundary marks the end of the Costa Dorada and the beginning of the Costa del Azahar, is SANT CARLES DE LA RÁPITA. Its huge natural harbour, supplemented by man-made sea-walls, serves a prosperous fishing fleet. A good deal of ship-building activity may be seen here, as well. But what makes Sant Carles (population about 10,000) different from all the other towns is its **main square.**

This gigantic plaza looks just the place for a coronation parade. It is so enormous, and the town itself so small, that there aren't enough shops and offices to fill its perimeter; many of the buildings are just private houses. The square was a city-planning brainstorm of Charles III, an eccentric 18th-century ruler who pictured Sant Carles as a port of international significance. The grandiose project died with him in 1788, but the legacy of his street plan and the melancholy square remain. Impertinently, the main road to Valencia goes right down the middle of Charles's freakish plaza.

Traditional fishing fleet occupies waterfront in Cambrils but tourists coexist and exploit nearby beaches.

Inland Excursions

Montserrat
(Barcelona, 62 km.)

For 700 years, pilgrims have been climbing the mighty rock formations to the monastery of Montserrat. Now that donkeys have been replaced by cable cars and excursion coaches, about a million people make the trip every year. The statistics don't say how many are pilgrims and how many are just sightseers, but one way or the other, visitors feel uplifted in this mountain redoubt.

Geographically and spiritually, Montserrat is the heart of Catalonia. The ancient Benedictine monastery, tucked into the rock, houses the patron of the Catalans—a 12th-century polychrome wood image of the Virgin Mary called **La Moreneta,** the little brown Madonna. Notice her nose: long, thin and pointed; it's the same nose you'll see on half the faces in the congregation. It's a thoroughly Catalan nose.

The brown madonna is so avidly venerated here that you may have to queue for 15 minutes for a look. The statue, in a niche above the basilica's high altar, is protected by glass. But a circle cut out of the shield permits the faithful to touch or kiss the image's outstretched right hand. Your visit may be delayed a minute or two while formally dressed newly-weds are ushered to the head of the line to pray and be photographed alongside La Moreneta (an unusual number of weddings take place in the pompous basilica, often witnessed by thousands of foreign tourists).

Tour companies run half-day and full-day excursions to Montserrat from Barcelona and all the major resorts of the Costa Dorada.

A highlight of any visit to Montserrat is its choir. The young choristers of the Escolanía, thought to be the oldest music-school in Europe, perform in the monastery at midday. The angelic voices sing as inspiringly as advertised.

A guided tour of the monastery concentrates on its **museum,** devoted to works of art and history. Several rooms cover "the Biblical East" through relics thousands of years old from Mesopotamia, Egypt and Palestine. Gold and silver chalices and reliquaries are on view. And the museum's art gallery owns a number of notable paintings, including a striking *Portrait of St. Jerome* by Caravaggio.

The monks here are rarely in view, busy as they are elsewhere with prayer, meditation, study in a 200,000-volume library, and down-to-earth labour. They make pottery, run a goldsmith's workshop and a printing plant, and distill a pleasant herbal liqueur called *Aromas de Montserrat.*

For a few pesetas, you can sample *Aromas* in the monastery's tourist bar, which also dispenses coffee and soft and hard drinks. It is one of a disconcertingly mundane array of shops and services for visitors. Montserrat has a hotel, a hairdressing salon, self-service restaurant and a souvenir supermarket.

The brisk commercial atmosphere disillusions some pilgrims, but the overall effect of Montserrat and its eerie mountains remains powerful.

In the basilica, with its eighton stone altar made of the mountain itself, sit and listen to the boys sing the *Virolai,* Montserrat's hymn. Perhaps you'll be able to distinguish some of the words—*Montserrat* and *la catalana terra.* The Catalan land and Montserrat have been inseparable

Symbol of Catalanism, Montserrat monastery is tucked into the rock.

for centuries. You'll begin to understand how when you hear the congregation join the choir in this anthem.

When you've seen one monastery, you have definitely not seen them all. The medieval fortress-monastery of Poblet contrasts sharply with Montserrat. Few tourists crowd Poblet, 45 kilometres northwest of Tarragona. While Montserrat clings to its granite

This powerful Cistercian monastery was founded more than 800 years ago by the count of Barcelona, Ramón Berenguer IV, as a gesture of thanksgiving for the reconquest of Catalonia from the Moors. The royal connections brought the monastery fame, fortune and historical importance. Poblet's church, as large as a cathedral, contains the **tombs** of the kings

mountain, Poblet sprawls upon a wide-open plateau amidst fertile hillsides. Montserrat's buildings, almost totally destroyed in 1811, were replaced by undistinguished architecture. Poblet's buildings were plundered and pillaged in 1835, but lovingly restored—and they have great architectural importance, as well as beauty.

of Aragon, suspended on unique low arches in the cross vault. Here lie James I the Conqueror (Jaime I el Conquistador), Peter the Ceremonious (Pedro el Ceremonioso), John I (Juan I) and his two wives, and Alphonse the Chaste (Alfonso el Casto). (Only fragments of the original sculpture were preserved, so the pantheon of today is a skilled reproduction.) Another outstanding example of alabaster sculpture is the **altarpiece** by the 16th-century artist Damia Forment. Tourists are guided through the most historic halls making up the monastic community.

The real appreciation of a monastic mood comes in the **cloister,** with its rose bushes

Beauty and tranquillity in medieval surroundings at Poblet monastery.

and four brooding poplars, the quiet relieved only by the trickling fountain and the twitter of birds. Beauty and serenity reign in this historic quadrangle.

Santes Creus

(Barcelona, 98 km.)

About 40 kilometres from Poblet—the route goes through the district market town of Valls (see p. 68)—another great monastery sprawls among the vineyards. The Cistercian monastery of Santes Creus was founded in the middle of the 12th century. While Poblet is a working monastery, Santes Creus has been preserved as a museum. Thus all buildings are on view here—from the dormitories to the kitchen.

The **cloister,** a pioneering work of Catalan Gothic design, dates from the beginning of the 14th century. Notice the stone carvings on the arches and in unexpected places on the walls: heraldic designs, animals, sometimes humorous faces.

The **church,** begun in 1174, is austere and powerful. The kings of Aragon and Catalonia were patrons of Santes Creus; the monastery's abbot was royal chaplain. And here, opposite the presbytery, are royal sepulchres. King Peter III the Great (Pedro el Grande) is buried here in a temple-within-in-a-church—a tall Gothic tabernacle. The royal remains **67** were interred in a Roman bath resting on four stone lions and covered by an elaborate alabaster tombstone.

In addition to several tombs of lesser grandeur, the monastery reveals its regal connections in the so-called "Royal Palace"—living quarters surrounding a perfect 14th-century patio of delicate arches and a finely sculpted staircase.

Human castle team assembles itself gingerly at breakneck speed.

Valls
(Barcelona, 105 km.)

The busy provincial town of Valls (population about 15,000) is famous throughout Catalonia for two odd superlatives. It produces the highest-rising human castles and the most delicious onions.

The *castellers* (see FOLKLORE, page 71) of Valls—known here as the *Xiquets* (pronounced SHEE-kets)—are looked up to both figuratively and literally. No other team in Catalonia has ever managed such skyscrapers of boys balanced atop men astride giants.

As for the onions—called *calçots*—they are gently cooked when very young, dipped in a special sauce, and consumed with grilled sausage or lamb. Summer tourists miss the boat, for this feast only takes place from about December to April.

The next best treat for visitors is *Firagost,* as the festivities of the first half of August are called. Farmers from the entire district bring their finest flowers and fruits to Valls for a tribute to the bounty of the earth. It's a lively time, with folk-dancing, fireworks and, of course, personal appearances by the *Xiquets*.

Vilafranca del Penedés
(Barcelona, 54 km.)

In the year 1217 the Catalonian parliament—the Cortes Catalanes—convened for the first time. The place: Vilafranca del Penedés, on a fertile plateau midway between Barcelona and Tarragona. Since then the population has grown tenfold, to 20,000. But the city still commands more fame than its size would justify. Thousands of tourists who come here by car or coach think of Vilafranca as Wine City. This is the home of Spain's most impressive **wine museum.**

You don't have to be a connoisseur, or even a drinker, to find fascination in the exhibits. Lively three-dimensional dioramas illustrate the business and pleasure of wine through the ages. You can see the actual wine presses which were crushing the grapes 2,000 years ago. And one hall displays glasses, bottles and jugs covering centuries of thirst. There is even an art gallery devoted to the vine and its ramifications.

The wine museum shares its quarters with the **Museu Municipal** (city museum) of Vilafranca, devoted primarily to geological exhibits and pre-historic finds. The building used to be a palace of the counts of Barcelona and the kings of Aragon.

Vilafranca del Penedés has one other enthusiasm. The local team of *castellers*—human pyramids—so captivates the citizens that in 1963 a monument was unveiled in their honour. It's right there in Plaça Jaume I, an interpretation of a five-story *pilar*; locally it's claimed to be among the world's tallest modern statues.

Several wine producers in the Penedés district invite tourists to visit their premises for an explanation of the production process and a sample of the end result. An impressive establishment at Sant Sadurní d'Anoia, the Codorniu caves, attracts many excursion coaches. From January to June, this one plant turns out thousands of bottles of "sparkling cellar wine" per day.

Andorra
(Barcelona, 220 km.)

Excursion firms all along the Costa Dorada advertise gruelling one-day trips to Andorra, **69** the 188-square-mile principality huddling between mountain peaks in the Pyrenees. With well over 200 kilometres of travel in each direction, not much time is left for sightseeing in tiny Andorra itself. In fact, most of the visit is devoted to shopping. Since Andorra is free of the taxes which afflict neighbouring countries, the price of almost

are almost universally understood, while English and German are most useful in the shops.

Aside from the crass business of bargain-hunting, take time for a stroll through ANDORRA LA VELLA, the capital. Most of the principality's permanent residents live there. Visit the Casa dels Valls, a 16th-century building in which

everything comes as a refreshing surprise. After 700 years of fiercely defended independence, the country's spectacular scenery now takes second place; most of today's visitors are heading straight for the bulging shops of Carrer Meritxell.

Andorra is the only country in which the official language **70** is Catalan. Spanish and French

Flag and escutcheon proclaim individuality of state of Andorra, protected by peaks of Pyrenees.

the country's parliament and court are housed. The nation's archives rest in a chest secured with six locks, the keys to which are held in the six parishes.

What to Do

Folklore

The stately *sardana*, the national dance of Catalonia, evokes an uncommon affection and interest among the people. The music may grate at first, because of its hints of Arabic woodwinds and the trills of Italian operetta. It also endures longer than one would have thought possible: just four lines of music repeated without mercy for up to ten minutes. This is a rugged workout for the dancers, who link hands, young and old together, friends or strangers, in an ancient type of round dance. Serious *sardana* dancers change into traditional light shoes—*alpargatas*—but anyone can join in. The musical instruments accompanying these floating but subtle exertions are a sort of oboe and a small flute and a small drum, the latter two played in tandem, one for each hand.

A dance for specialists is the *Ball dels Bastons* (dance of the sticks) which enlivens many fiestas. Highly trained young men or boys in costume perform an intricate and potentially somewhat dangerous stick-dance, reminiscent of fencing and jousting.

Castellers are the men and boys who climb upon each other's shoulders to form human towers. The sport requires the skill of the mountain climber and the tightrope walker, plus trust and teamwork to the extreme. One false move could tumble the whole pyramid.

The *castellers* will always climb barefoot. The unsung, unseen heroes are the behemoths on the bottom layer. The most pampered participant is the local boy—perhaps only six years old—who has been trained to scamper to the summit like a monkey. When he reaches the top of the pyramid, the *enxaneta* (weathercock) releases one hand for a couple of seconds to wave a victory sign. The crowd cheers. Deftly, the castle comes apart from the top down.

During religious processions and other combinations of solemnity and fireworks, many towns parade their giant effigies *(Gegants* and *Cabezudos)*. Skilled crews hidden beneath these figures, which are three times human size, balance the heavy statues and even make them dance. At some festivals, firecracker squads reminiscent of Chinese dragon impersona-

Earnest musicians set the pace for sardana *dancing in Barcelona.*

tors plough through the crowds, generating blinding glare and deafening noise. No one finds it incongruous when all this is followed by a plodding procession of little girls and old women holding lighted tapers and religious banners. The quick-changing moods are contagious.

The Bullfight

Nothing is more uniquely Spanish—or incomprehensible to the foreigner—than the *fiesta brava,* the bullfight. If you've never experienced this spectacle, you may want to seize the chance on your visit to the Coșta Dorada. Although bullfighting is not a particularly Catalonian pursuit it is extremely popular, particularly in Barcelona, which has two bullrings.

Understand from the beginning that the bullfight is not regarded as a sport. A sport is a contest between equals; in bullfighting the odds are weighted heavily against the bull. The *corrida* is a ritualistic preparation for the bull's death. Yet, every time the *torero* enters the ring, he knows his own life is in danger. (Call him a *torero,* please, and not *toreador,* which you may have picked up—erroneously—from Bizet's *Carmen.*) In the first *tercio* (third) of the fight, the matador meets the fierce bull, takes his measure and begins to tire him using the big red and yellow *capote.*

In the second *tercio* the *picador,* a mounted spearman in Sancho Panza costume, lances the bull's shoulder muscles, and the deft *banderilleros* stab darts into the animal's shoulders.

At last the matador returns to taunt the bull with the small, dark-red *muleta* cape, eventually dominating the beast. Finally, as the bull awaits the death he must now sense is inevitable, the *torero* lunges for the kill.

The bull staggers to its knees, bringing the corrida to an end.

You may be upset or fascinated or simply confused by an afternoon at the *plaza de toros*. But you will have witnessed a violent act which at times contains touching beauty. With luck, you'll come to understand why this ballet of death is considered an art form in Spain.

Flamenco

Spain's best-known entertainment, after the bullfight, is flamenco—throbbing guitars, stamping heels and songs that gush from the soul. Many of the songs resemble the wailing chants of Arab music, which may be a strong clue to flamenco's origins. Throughout the region, flamenco shows are popular tourist attractions.

There are two main groups of songs: one, bouncier and more cheerful, is known as the *cante chico* (a light tune). The second group of songs, called *cante jondo,* deals with love, death, all the human drama, in the slow, piercing style of the great flamenco singers.

But it's the *cante chico* you'll hear at the nightclub floorshow called the *tablao flamenco.* Less dramatic and soulsearching, the *cante chico* is 73 basically lighthearted but can be philosophical and touching. It all makes for a big night out with excitement and colour. And perhaps you'll come away with a feeling for the real flamenco: an ageless beauty in a dramatic ruffle dress, clapping hands as fast as a humming-bird flaps its wings, defying an arrogant dark man chanting with his eyes half-closed.

Shopping

Shopping Hours

Along the coast most shops are open from about 9 a.m. to 2 p.m. and again from 4 to 8 or 10 p.m.

A significant exception: the big, non-stop department stores of Barcelona, which disregard the siesta tradition.

(Bars and cafés normally remain open from around 8 a.m. until midnight or later, with no afternoon break.)

Best Buys

Catalonian ceramics can be primitive or sophisticated, but they're usually quite original. Note the cheerful colours on the sleek modern bowls, which resemble Scandinavian dishware, and the subtle innovations in traditional pots and vases. Decorative tiles can be artistic or just witty with slogans in the Catalan language.

An intensive cottage industry along the coast produces leatherwork, mainly handbags and items of clothing. The quality of the leather and the workmanship is erratic and so is the style, but good buys can be found if you can spare the time to search for them.

Shoes often cost less in Spain than elsewhere in Europe but the workmanship of cheap models is unimpressive. Stylish shoes and boots can be top-class but expensive.

Embroidery, lacework and woven goods such as rugs and bedspreads are produced in coastal villages which keep alive the old patterns and skills. Notice the women of the knitting circles hiding from the hot sun; their products are often on sale in the local shops.

Jewellery, either simple modern designs or traditional styles with lots of silver or gold filigree, can include bargains for the knowledgeable.

For less expansive budgets, there are records of Catalan music—the *sardana* played by those reed bands, or emotional choral works—to remind you always of your holiday.

Or local glasswork, such as the *porróns,* from which wine is projected through the air to the consumer—or which just look intriguing on a shelf.

Or wooden candlesticks in locally carved designs.

Or vaguely snobbish miniature reproductions of Leonardo da Vinci inventions.

Among "best buys" of any trip to Spain are alcohol and tobacco. These are so cheap, by other European and American standards, that there's no need for duty-free shops. Many famous foreign drinks are bottled in Catalonia under licence, and cost the consumer a fraction of the price at home. But for a souvenir gift, buy a bottle of one of the regional liqueurs.

Souvenirs

If you insist on buying "traditional" Spanish souvenirs, there's no shortage of shops overflowing with mock bull-fighter swords from Toledo, inlaid Moorish-style chess sets, imitation antique pistols, bullfight posters (with or without your own name imprinted as a star matador), statuettes of Don Quixote, and the typical Spanish *bota,* or wineskin (which is likely to be lined with plastic).

Antiques

You'll have to leave the tourist areas to find any amazing old trinkets at bargain prices. But even in a resort you may come across an appealing piece of old ironwork or hand carving at a relatively sensible price. At very least you can always take home a rusty old door

key suitable for a haunted house, or a kitchen iron of genuine pre-electric vintage.

Antique shopping is made easy in Barcelona, where many shops are concentrated in the ancient streets around the cathedral. Dealers carry antiques as well as reproductions of antiques; sometimes the dividing line becomes blurred.

Shopping Tips

Barcelona, with its fashionable shops, offers variety and quality, but no single street or neighbourhood will satisfy your window-shopping. The commercial area is so extensive that you might have to walk miles to compare quality and value.

Prices in tourist resorts almost always exceed those in the big cities or inland towns,

and they tend to vary from shop to shop, too.

Occasionally, you'll see a notice of sales—*rebajas* (or *rebaixes* in Catalan)—in shop windows. While legitimate sales do take place, usually at the end of the season, you'll have to be a bit cautious.

The Spanish government levies a value added tax (called "IVA") on most items. Tourists from abroad will be refunded the IVA they pay on purchases over a stipulated amount. To obtain the rebate, you have to fill out a form, provided by the shop. The shop keeps one copy; the three others must be presented at the customs on departure, together with the goods. The rebate will then be forwarded by the shop to your home address.

Museums

Barcelona alone counts more than 40 museums. This listing of Costa Dorada museums covers only those institutions of greatest general interest.

Most Spanish museums are open from Tuesday to Saturday from about 10 a.m. to 1.30 or 2 p.m., and 6 to 8 p.m., and Sundays from 10 a.m. to 2 p.m.; closed on Mondays and certain holidays.

Barcelona

Museu Arqueològic (Archaeological Museum). Art and relics dug up in the Barcelona area as well as elsewhere in Spain—prehistoric implements, Carthaginian necklaces, Roman mosaics (Carrer de Lleida, at the foot of Montjuïc; see also p. 35).

Museu d'Art de Catalunya (Museum of Catalonian Art). Top-priority museum, with a beautifully arranged and displayed collection of medieval religious art, all housed in a mock palace (Palau Nacional, Montjuïc; see p. 35).

Museu de Cera (Wax Museum). This one is commercial and more expensive. Three hundred wax effigies of historical, contemporary and fictional figures (Rambla).

Colecció Cambó (Cambó Collection). Paintings by Raphael and Titian, Goya and El Greco, Rubens and van Dyck, in an elegant palace (Palau de Pedralbes; see also p. 46).

Museu Picasso (Carrer de Montcada, 15). From early scribblings to most mature tri-

Barcelona boasts great collection of medieval art. Opposite: shops sell antiques and original pottery.

umphs, the life's work of the great Spanish painter is laid out in three noble mansions of Old Barcelona (see pp. 40–41).

Museu de l'Indumentaria (Costume Museum). More than 4,000 items showing the **77**

evolution of fashion from the 16th century to the present (Carrer de Montcada, 12).

Museu d'Art Modern (Museum of Modern Art). Nineteenth and 20th-century paintings by Catalan artists in the Parc de la Ciutadella (see also pp. 44–45).

Museu Marítim (Maritime Museum). Medieval shipyard (Drassanes) converted into repository of full-sized and miniature souvenirs from the high seas, with replica of Columbus's flagship *Santa María* in the harbour (see pp. 37–38).

Fundació Joan Miró (Joan Miró Foundation). Paintings and sculptures, mostly by Miró, exhibited in brilliant galleries and gardens in the Parc de Montjuïc (see p. 35).

Museu Frederic Marés (Federico Marés Museum). Right next to the Cathedral in Carrer Comtes, a vast collection of ancient religious sculptures.

Palau de Pedralbes (Pedralbes Palace). 1920s palace fit for a King (Alfonso XIII). See also p. 46.

Poble Espanyol (Spanish Village). Instructive, imaginary all-Spanish town without children, dogs, or characters (on Montjuïc).

Museu Militar (Military Museum). Military souvenirs —uniforms, castle maquettes, toy soldiers, real guns—in a mainly 18th-century fortress atop Montjuïc.

Museu d'Història de la Ciutat (Museum of the History of the City). Built by chance right on top of Barcelona's richest archaeological digs in Plaça del Rei, this museum's skilfully lit basement is an archaeology lover's delight (see p. 26).

Museu del Monestir de Pedralbes (Museum of the Monastery of Pedralbes). Main attraction of this museum is a collection of beautiful wall paintings by Ferrer Bassa from the 14th century (see also p. 46).

Tarragona

Museu Arqueològic (Archaeological Museum). Statues, mosaics and medaillons from Tarragona's Roman era. (Note: Adjoining **Pretori Romà** with additional ancient objects.)

Necròpoli i Museu Paleocristià (Necropolis and Paleo-Christian Museum). Tarragona's early Christians were buried here in style and grace.

Passeig Arqueològic (Archaeological promenade). City walls and watch towers amid meticulously tended gardens. Open until midnight in summer. (Roman Forum, another outdoor attraction, also operates floodlit in summer.)

Rent-a-burro: how to make a child happy. The donkey's smiling, too.

For Children

Barcelona Zoo. As pleasant and instructive a zoo as you'll find anywhere in the world.

Poble Espanyol, Barcelona. Simulated Spanish town recreating architecture from all provinces in one slightly confusing ensemble. Watch a woodcarver chisel a statuette, a glassblower make a vase.

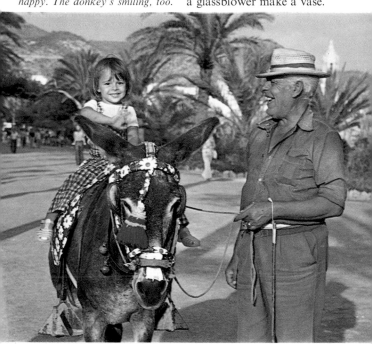

Boat Trips. Round Barcelona harbour in a launch, for instance, for a close-up inspection of a busy port. Excursion firms also operate day-trips by bus and boat to Costa Brava.

Fun Fairs (Amusement Parks). Two big ones in Barcelona, on Montjuïc and Tibidabo. Noise and gaiety along with fine views of the city and sea.

Güell Park. Gaudí's zany whimsicality charms children, who especially admire his optical illusions. Free.

Barcelona Maritime Museum. The history of sailing, from Roman anchors to model of nuclear-propelled ship.

Santa María replica. Part of the Maritime Museum, a full-size model of Columbus's flagship is moored in the port nearby, available for boarding during the daytime.

Burro Safari. Travel agencies mobilize donkeys for tourist outings.

Tartana Excursions. A country trip in a horse-drawn cart, as devised by travel agencies.

Bloodless Bullfights. Mock *corridas* with baby bulls and audience participation. Some agencies include "champagne" and dancing.

Safari Excursion. Coach tours make a half-day outing to and through Rioleón Safari, where wild animals roam free. Near El Vendrell (Tarragona).

Festivals

Religious and civic holidays are so frequent in Spain that the odds favour your witnessing a fiesta during your holiday, wherever you may be:

80 *Balloons and bouncing balls prove simple pleasures are usually best.*

February
L'Ametlla de Mar   *Festes de la Candelària*. Religious procession, regatta.

Vilanova i la Geltrú   *Festes de "Les Comparses"*. Folklore and *"battle of sweets"*; 40 tons of sweets are consumed.

March or April
Montserrat
Poblet   *Setmana Santa* (Holy Week) ceremonies. Processions and other observances in all towns.

April
Barcelona   *Diada de Sant Jordì*. St. George's Day, coinciding with Cervantes Day, a Book Fair, and the Day of Lovers. Animation and colour.

May
Badalona   *Festes de Primavera i Sant Anastasi*. Spring Festival and St. Anastasius' Day. Exhibition of roses.

Calella   *Festes de Primavera*. Spring Festival. Folk-dancing competition, old car parade, marching bands.

May or June
Sitges   *Festa del Corpus Christi*. Streets carpeted with flowers. Music, dancing, fireworks.

June
Calella   *"Aplec" de Sardanas*. Catalonia's most important folk-dance festival.

July
Arenys de Mar   *Festa major de Sant Zenón*. Celebrations asea and ashore. Folklore.

August
Valls   *Festes del Firagost* (Assumption). Harvest celebration, folklore, religious procession.

Vilafranca del Penedés   *Festa major de Sant Félix, mártir*. Religious procession. Folklore featuring "human castles".

September
Barcelona   *Festes de la Mercè*. Theatre, music.

Tarragona   *Festes de Santa Tecla* (St. Thecla). Religious and folkloric spectacles.

October
Sitges   *Festa de la Varema* (Grape-harvest festival). Tastings and dance.

Nightlife

Barcelona swings. So do the major resorts. Almost anywhere tourists alight along the Costa Dorada they find a conglomeration of bars, discothèques and *boîtes*. There's really no excuse except exhaustion for spending an evening slumped before the television in your hotel lounge.

Tour agencies along the coast run a Saturday-night excursion to Barcelona to admire the illuminated fountains of Montjuïc and see Flamenco dancers in small specialized restaurants. There are two basic kinds of Flamenco (see p. 73), and the animated *cante chico* is the version usually performed in *tablaos*. Although Flamenco is essentially an art of Southern Spain and seen to its best effect there, Barcelona attracts many of the great performers.

Another excursion by coach takes in the most elegant floorshows in Barcelona. Normally the all-inclusive price includes dinner and a quota of drinks.

Organized barbecue evenings are a popular rustic substitute for the big-city nightclub tour. Travel agencies

take coachloads of tourists from the resorts to a regional beauty spot where plenty of food, wine and music are supplied.

Big and little towns along the coast have their discothèques and flamenco shows. In fine weather it's a novelty to escape from deafening smoke-filled rooms into deafening open-air nightspots. There is something special about dancing under the moon and stars.

Concerts, Opera, Ballet

Local or visiting orchestras and choirs provide a steady diet for Barcelona music-lovers.

The city's Opera House, the Gran Teatre del Liceu, was described as the finest theatre in the world when it opened in 1857. Famous opera and ballet companies appear there every year between November and May. Most of its seats belong to subscribers, so it may be difficult for the casual ticket-hunter to obtain seats.

Major concerts also take place at the wildly *art nouveau*

Night on the Costa Dorada: bars, discos, restaurants for all tastes.

Palau de la Música Catalana.

Recitals, including occasional jazz concerts, are held in the stark surroundings of the 14th-century Església de Santa Maria del Mar.

Catalans are deeply dedicated to music, so you may chance upon a concert in any resort town—perhaps the local choir performing in the parish church or the town cinema.

Theatre, Films

Most of Barcelona's dozen theatres seem to specialize in musicals and farces, but straight plays—in Spanish or Catalan—are also presented.

Almost all the films shown commercially in Spain have been dubbed into Spanish. Depending on the location of the cinema and success of the film, the prices of seats vary (see p. 100).

Fiestas

Village fetes, which occur with great frequency, can provide rousing spectacles, music, folk dancing. But Spaniards are very casual about fireworks, so beware of the more explosive parts of town.

Wining and Dining

When in Spain, try some Spanish food. This advice is not so ludicrous as it may seem. You could easily spend a fortnight's holiday in Barcelona or on the Costa Dorada subsisting on the anonymous international food in your hotel. What a shame.

Spanish cooking varies drastically from region to region.*

To many visitors, a favourite dish is *gazpacho* (pronounced gath-PAT-cho), a chilled, highly flavoured soup to which chopped tomatoes, peppers, cucumbers, onions and sippets (croutons) are added to taste—a rousing refresher on a hot summer day.

Another classic Spanish dish, *paella* (pronounced pie-ALE-

---

* For a comprehensive food list, ask at your bookshop for the Berlitz Spanish-English/English-Spanish dictionary, or the Berlitz EUROPEAN MENU READER.

84

ya), originated just down the coast in Valencia. It's named after the black iron pan in which the saffron rice is cooked. To this the cook adds whatever inspires him at the moment—squid, sausage, shrimp, rabbit, chicken, mussels, onion, peppers, peas, beans, tomatoes, garlic... Authentically, *paella* is served at lunchtime, cooked to order (about half an hour). Some Spaniards consider it a first course; others dig into it for the whole meal.

Catalan Cuisine

Esqueixada (pronounced es-kay-SHA-da) is a stimulating salad of cod, beans, pickled onions and tomato.

Xató (pronounced sha-TO) *de Sitges* is a related, but more complicated salad including anchovies, tunny fish or cod and a hot sauce made of olive oil, vinegar, red pepper, diced anchovies, garlic and ground almonds.

Pa amb tomàquet goes well with any salad. Peasant-style bread, in huge slices, is smeared with fresh tomato and grilled; it comes out a sort of primitive cousin of a pizza.

Escudella is considered a winter-time dish, but out of season you may come across the hearty broth containing beans, pasta, a chunk of sausage and a slice of meatloaf.

Butifarra is one of several varieties of sausage much appreciated in Catalonia. One famous species of sausage comes from the town of Vic.

Rovellons are enormous wild mushrooms which mark the start of autumn on the Costa Dorada. They're cooked with garlic and parsley, eaten with sausage or alone.

Pollo al ast (barbecued chicken) is grilled and basted on the spit, usually outside a restaurant so that the aroma lures customers inside.

Riz parellada, a Costa Do-

Rushed from the farm, fruits and vegetables temptingly displayed.

rada refinement of *paella,* is a gourmand's dream. The kitchen will have removed all the shells and bones from the seafood and meat before this feast is cooked, so it can be gulped down without mess or delay.

Fish in general makes up a substantial part of the local diet. Mostly it is just grilled and served with a salad and fried potatoes. In more sophisticated restaurants, you'll be offered elaborate variations with subtle sauces. No matter how primitive or elegant the place, the raw materials are likely to be first-rate.

Romesco is the fish sauce from Tarragona, envied and imitated in other Costa Dorada towns. This red sauce tastes right at home beside the Mediterranean in the company of fried fish and shellfish. The cooks of Tarragona are very coy when asked for the recipe, but key ingredients would appear to be red pepper, olive oil, garlic, bread crumbs and ground almonds.

Calçotada, an even more provincial dish, comes from Valls—tender baby onions in what's claimed to be the most irresistible combination of vegetables, meat and spices in all of Catalonia.

Sweets: The pastries of the Costa Dorada will destroy your diet. Just look in a bakery window; you don't have to know the names. One is more delectable than the next, crowned with nuts, custard, dried fruits, meringue, chocolate or powder sugar.

Crema Catalana, made of eggs, sugar, milk and cinnamon, is cooked to a more solid consistency than its Spanish cousin, *flan,* and it has a caramel-glaze topping.

Breakfast

In Spain breakfast is an insignificant meal—just an eye-opener to keep one alive until a huge and late lunch. A typical Costa Dorada breakfast consists of a cup of coffee and pastry. Breakfast coffee *(café con leche)* is half coffee, half hot milk. If it tastes too foreign to you, many bars and restaurants stock milder instant coffee, as well. Also in deference to foreign habits, *desayuno completo* is now available in most hotels and some cafés: orange juice, eggs, toast and coffee.

Returning to the subject of breakfast pastry, two types are worth a try. *Ensaimadas* are large fluffy sweet rolls dusted with sugar, a Balearic islands speciality also popular in Catalonia. *Churros* are fritters, often made before your eyes by a contraption which shoots the batter into boiling oil. If you *don't* dunk *churros* in your coffee, everyone will stare. (*Churros* with very thick hot chocolate is a popular afternoon snack in Spain.)

Restaurants

All Spanish restaurants are officially graded by forks, not stars. One fork is the lowest grade, five forks the élite. But ratings are awarded according to the facilities available, not the quality of the food. Many forks on the door guarantee higher prices but not necessarily better cooking.

Spanish restaurants usually offer a *menú del día* (day's special). This usually lists three courses available with bread and wine at a reasonable set price. But the *menú* is not always a bargain; in fact, it might even work out to cost more than the sum of its parts. Add up the *à la carte* prices to be certain. On the other hand, in country or working-class restaurants, the *menú* is

often the favourite of the regular clients, and cheap.

Normally, menu prices are "all-inclusive"—including all taxes and service charge. But it's still customary to leave a tip. Ten percent is acceptable, 15 percent is generous.

All restaurants, for the record, announce that an official complaints book is available to dissatisfied clients.

All that food but too busy to eat: rush hour in a Barcelona kitchen.

Meal times tend to be later than in most European countries. Restaurants serve lunch from about 1 to 3.30 p.m. and dinner from about 8.30 to 11. **87**

Resort hotels may serve dinner earlier for the convenience of foreign guests.

One hint for economy: order *vino de la casa* (house wine). It may be served in an anonymous bottle, a colourful ceramic carafe or even in a mislabelled second-hand bottle. But it's almost bound to be tolerably good and will cost less than half the price of a brand-name bottle.

Foreign Restaurants

Barcelona is reasonably well provided with restaurants featuring foreign cuisines. They include French, Italian, German and Chinese restaurants. In addition Barcelona has many fine restaurants devoted to regional cooking from the various gourmet regions of Spain.

Most resort centres also have eating places aiming at foreign palates. The restaurants enjoy varying degrees of authenticity.

Bars and Cafés

Open-air cafés are one of the pleasures of the region. A cup of coffee buys you a ringside seat for as long as you care to dawdle.

Bar and café bills include service charges, but small tips are the custom. Prices are usually 10 or 15 percent higher if you're served at a table rather than at the bar.

Bodegas are wine-cellars. In resort towns many popular tourist bars have been designed to create the atmosphere of casks and barrels.

Merenderos are beach restaurants, serving simple but tasty food.

Tapas

A *tapa* is a bite-sized morsel of food—meatballs, olives, fried-fish chunks, shellfish, seafood, vegetable salad; it can be almost anything edible. The word *tapa* means "lid" and comes from the old custom of giving a bite of food with a drink, the food being served on a saucer covering the top of the glass like a lid. Nowadays, sadly, the custom of giving away the *tapa* is all but nonexistent. But the idea of selling *tapas* is stronger than ever. Some bars, called *tascas,* specialize in the snack trade. Instead of sitting down to a formal meal in a restaurant you can wander into a *tapa* bar, point to the items you like and eat your way down the counter. One helping is called a *porción*. For a large serving of any given *tapa*, ask for a *ración*. If that's too much for you, order a *media-ración*. Caution: it's quite possible to spend more for a meal of *tapas* than for a good, conventional dinner.

Wines and Spirits

Both provinces of the Costa Dorada—Barcelona and Tarragona—produce good wine.

Priorato is a well-known red wine of the region. Tarragona wines are notable in white or rosé. Penedés can be red or white. In Sitges a dessert wine, malmsey (*malvasía* in Spanish), is produced. And the Penedés region is a major source of the world's best selling white sparkling wine, called *cava*.

Don't give a thought to "winemanship", or matching wits with the wine waiter to choose just the right vintage. When the average Spaniard sits down to a meal, he just orders *"vino"*, and it means *red* wine to the average waiter. Often served chilled, this house wine can go with fish or meat or anything. Relax and enjoy the unpretentiousness.

There is no social misdemeanour implied in diluting your wine if you wish, particularly on a hot day. The addition of *gaseosa*, a cheap fizzy lemonade, turns red wine into an imitation of *sangría*. (Real

As in all Mediterranean countries, outdoor cafés prosper in Catalonia. **89**

sangría, however, is a mixture of red wine, lemon and orange juice, brandy, mineral water, ice and slices of fruit—rather like punch and very popular in hot summer.)

If you're not in the mood for wine at all, have no qualms about ordering beer or a soft drink or mineral water. No one will turn up a snobbish nose.

You may consider Spanish brandy too heavy or sweet for your taste, compared with French cognac. But it's very cheap—often the same price as a soft drink.

A word about prices: if you insist on drinking imported Scotch or bourbon, expect to pay plenty. However, an enormous range of familiar spirits and liqueurs are available at very low prices because they are made under licence in Spain. Look around a wine shop to see just how cheap some brands are.

A last word to alert you to a non-alcoholic drink you might not have noticed. *Horchata de chufa* is a very Spanish refresher, possibly first imported by the Moors. It's made from a fruity, wrinkled little nut with a sweet taste, similar to an almond. *Horchaterías,* bars specializing in this popular cold drink, often have terraces and also serve all kinds of ice-cream.

To help you order...

Could we have a table?	**¿Nos puede dar una mesa?**		
Do you have a set menu?	**¿Tiene un menú del día?**		
I'd like a/an/some...	**Quisiera...**		

beer	**una cerveza**	milk	**leche**
bread	**pan**	mineral water	**agua mineral**
coffee	**un café**	napkin	**una servilleta**
condiments	**los condimentos**	potatoes	**patatas**
cutlery	**los cubiertos**	rice	**arroz**
dessert	**un postre**	salad	**una ensalada**
fish	**pescado**	sandwich	**un bocadillo**
fruit	**fruta**	soup	**sopa**
glass	**un vaso**	sugar	**azúcar**
ice-cream	**un helado**	tea	**un té**
meat	**carne**	(iced) water	**agua (fresca)**
menu	**la carta**	wine	**vino**

90

...and read the menu

aceitunas	olives	guisantes	peas
ajo	garlic	helado	ice-cream
albaricoques	apricots	higos	figs
albóndigas	meatballs	huevo	eggs
almejas	baby clams	jamón	ham
anchoas	anchovies	judías	beans
anguila	eel	langosta	spiny lobster
arroz	rice	langostino	prawn
asado	roast	lenguado	sole
atún	tunny (tuna)	limón	lemon
bacalao	codfish	lomo	loin
besugo	sea bream	manzana	apple
bistec	beef steak	mariscos	shellfish
boquerones	fresh anchovies	mejillones	mussels
caballa	mackerel	melocotón	peach
calamares	squid	merluza	hake
(a la romana)	(deep fried)	naranja	orange
callos	tripe	ostras	oysters
cangrejo	crab	pastel	cake
caracoles	snails	pescado	fish
cebollas	onions	pescadilla	whiting
cerdo	pork	pez espada	swordfish
champiñones	mushrooms	pimiento	green pepper
chorizo	a spicy pork sausage	piña	pineapple
		plátano	banana
chuleta	chops	pollo	chicken
cordero	lamb	postre	dessert
dorada	sea-bass	pulpitos	baby octopus
ensalada	salad	queso	cheese
entremeses	hors-d'oeuvre	salchichón	salami
estofado	stew	salmonete	red mullet
filete	fillet	salsa	sauce
flan	caramel mould	sandía	watermelon
frambuesas	raspberries	sopa	soup
fresas	strawberries	ternera	veal
frito	fried	tortilla	omelet
galletas	biscuits (cookies)	tostada	toast
		trucha	trout
gambas	shrimp	uvas	grapes
granadas	pomegranates	verduras	vegetables

Sports and Other Activities

Facilities vary from zero along isolated stretches to the elaborate bars and changing rooms of the big resorts.

Deck-chairs and umbrellas can be hired everywhere for a reasonable price. Air mattresses *(colchoneta),* for sunbathing and swimming, are another matter. It may well work out cheaper to buy your own for the season.

Vast sand beaches make the Costa Dorada a natural winner for holiday-makers inclined to water sports. The mild climate, moreover, extends the season for sports ashore. And if it should rain, the indoor sports provide exciting diversion, whether you play table tennis or watch Basques scoop up a bullet-fast *pelota.*

Here's a run-down of sports to choose from:

Beach Pursuits

Along much of the coast, golden sand slopes gently into a calm sea. The angle is less dependably gradual north-east of Barcelona; be alert for undercurrents. With few exceptions, lifeguards do not exist. But in many resorts first-aid stations are established on the main beaches.

Boating and Sailing

If you arrive in your own yacht, you'll find the facilities you need at any of these boating centres: Barcelona, Garraf, Vilanova i la Geltrú, Torredembarra, Tarragona, Salou, Cambrils, Sant Carles de la Rápita, Arenys de Mar.

If you've left your yacht at home but would like to hire a boat on the spot, many resorts can come up with sailing boats. It usually depends upon local beach and sea conditions. Small fibre-glass dinghies are perfectly safe for sailing just off shore. If you plan to do much sailing on your holiday, try to negotiate a cheaper bulk rate.

For the less adventurous or less affluent, there remains the *patines* (paddle boat). This sea-borne bicycle built for two can

of age on the coast. Equipment and instructors are available in many resorts.

Down to the sea in bathing suits, or all rigged up in a parachute to keep up with latest holiday sport.

Boardsailing, also known as windsurfing and windgliding —combining the speed of sailing with the thrill of tightrope walking—has come

be as unglamorous as an 1890s bathing costume, but it will take you far from the crowds. Check the prices before you embark. **93**

Water-Skiing

Increased fuel costs have pushed this sport into the luxury class.

In some resorts, an exciting airborne variation—kite-skiing—is attracting great attention. Definitely not for the faint-hearted.

Fishing

In all resorts incxpensive rods and reels are sold.

Deep-sea-style fishing is a logistical problem; if you can organize a group you may be able to hire a boat. There are no facilities for renting equipment.

For all information and licences, consult the local office of the Instituto Nacional para la Conservación de la Naturaleza (ICONA):

Barcelona: Carrer Sabino de Arana, 22.

Tarragona: Avda. de Catalunya, 22-E.

Underwater Fishing

This increasingly popular sport requires a licence, issued by the local Comandancia de Marina (Maritime Authorities). You may use a snorkel tube and mask along with mechanical harpoon. Underwater fishing with scuba oxygen equipment or air guns is strictly not allowed. Incidentally, if you should come upon archaeological relics in your undersea travels, remember that it is forbidden to collect these specimens.

Golf

Some golf courses are open all-year-round on the Costa Dorada, mostly near Barcelona.

- Real Club de Golf El Prat,

Tennis

Many hotels along the coast either have their own courts or can provide access for their guests to a local tennis club.

The Spanish sun is shining for the fishers on the quayside as for sedate golfers on the beautiful green near Barcelona.

in El Prat de Llobregat (near Barcelona airport). 27 holes.
- Club de Golf de San Cugat, near Sant Cugat del Vallés. 18 holes.
- Club de Golf Terramar, Sitges. Nine holes.

Horse-Riding

Some resort travel agencies advertise riding excursions with transport to and from a ranch, a few hours of riding, and a country meal.

Hunting and Shooting

Two areas of unusual interest for hunters in the southern part of Catalonia: the Ebro Delta and the rugged mountain zone west of Tortosa.

The Ebro Delta, the marshy peninsula facing Amposta, is considered one of the dozen best waterfowl spots in Spain, and Spain claims Europe's best

Tortosa and Beceite passes. This is one of the refuges of the Spanish mountain goat, a rare species in modern times. Hunting there is very severely controlled.

Otherwise, the Costa Dorada area is inhabited by unexceptional quantities of rabbit, hare and partridge. The small game season opens on October 12 and closes in February.

waterfowl hunting. The season begins in October and lasts to mid-March. For information and the actual hunting licence apply to the Instituto Nacional para la Conservación de la Naturaleza (ICONA), Avda. de Catalunya, 22-E, Tarragona.

The same ICONA office can answer your questions on the national hunting reserve of the

Skiing

Yes, skiing—on snow. Sophisticated winter resorts flourish from December to April in the Catalonian Pyrenees, within a hundred miles or so of Barcelona. The Direcció General issues a detailed booklet on winter sports in Catalonia.

Just Looking

Among spectator sports, football is Spain's greatest passion. Barcelona supports two major teams—Espanyol and Barcelona (affectionately known as *Barça*). *Barça's* stadium can seat about 90,000 spectators—almost the entire population of Tarragona

Popular indoor sports are

For a rousingly different experience, go to a *frontón* to watch the Basque ball game, *pelota,* called in Basque *jai-alai.* You'll catch on to the rules fairly early in the game, though the betting system which engrosses most of the audience may remain mysterious. Bookies in blue jackets negotiate with their clients by hand signals and slang, transmitting

Jai-alai *speed-merchants* (opposite) *thrill the crowds. Some* (above) *prefer a slower pace.*

basketball, boxing and wrestling.

Greyhounds *(galgos)* race at various *canódromos.* Betting is permitted.

receipts inside tennis balls. Even the referee, on the dangerous side of the protective fence, has been known to place a discreet bet during the match. The tireless players use woven straw scoops to combine the functions of glove and catapult, snagging the whizzing ball and blasting it back against the far wall.

97

BLUEPRINT for a Perfect Trip

How to Get There

If the choice of ways to go is bewildering, the complexity of fares and regulations can be downright stupefying. A reliable travel agent, up to date on the latest zigs and zags, can suggest which plan is best for your timetable and budget.

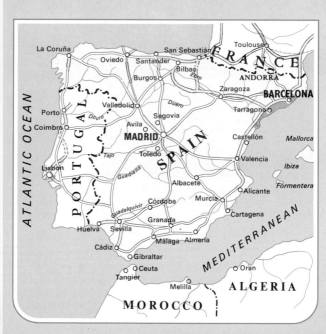

BY AIR

Scheduled flights

Barcelona Airport (see p. 102) is linked by regular flights from many European and certain overseas cities. Connecting service from cities throughout Europe and North Africa operates via Madrid's airport, which is the main point of entry to Spain for transatlantic and inter-continental travellers. The flight from London to Barcelona takes about 2 hours, from New York, approximately 8 hours.

Charter flights and package tours

From the U.K. and Ireland: Many companies operate all-in package tours, which include flight, hotel and meals; check carefully to make sure that you are not liable to any surcharges. British travel agents offer guarantees in case of bankruptcy or cancellation by the hotels or airlines. Most recommend insurance, too, for tourists who are forced to cancel because of illness or accident.

If you prefer to arrange your own accommodation and do not mind having to restrict your holiday to either one or two weeks, you can take advantage of the many charter flights that are available.

From North America: Most charter flights operate to Madrid or the Costa del Sol. If extensions are offered, it is possible to visit Barcelona and the Costa Dorada independently. Barcelona is often featured on package tours combining Majorca or the Costa del Sol.

BY ROAD

The main access road from France to Barcelona is at the eastern side of the Pyrenees, on the toll motorway (expressway), or via the more scenic coastal road. You could also travel via Toulouse and cross the Spanish border at Puigcerdà near Andorra and from there take the N-152 to Barcelona, or go via Pau (France) to Candanchú and Sara-gossa and/or Lleida (Lérida). There is a long distance ferry service between Plymouth and Santander in northern Spain (a 24-hour trip); from Santander, follow the N-240 to Barcelona.

Express **coach services** operate between London and Barcelona, with frequent departure in summer. You can travel by coach as part of a package holiday from London.

BY RAIL

The *Barcelona–Talgo* links Paris with Barcelona in about 11½ hours. For most other connections you'll have to change trains at Port Bou. Seat and sleeper reservations are compulsory on most Spanish trains.

Both *Inter-Rail* and *Rail Europ Senior* cards are valid in Spain, as is the *Eurailpass* for non-European residents (sign up before you leave home).

Visitors from abroad can buy the *RENFE (Red Nacional de los Ferrocarriles Española,* the Spanish National Railways) *Tourist Card* for a reasonable price, valid for unlimited rail travel within the country for periods of 8, 15 or 22 days (1st and 2nd classes available).

When to Go

Sunbathers enjoy the beaches of the Costa Dorada for about six months of the year; the rest of the time the mild climate still provides a pleasant break for visitors from northern Europe.

The accompanying chart deals specifically with the climate of Barcelona, damper than Tarragona and intermediate beach areas.

		J	F	M	A	M	J	J	A	S	O	N	D
average daily	°F	55	57	60	65	71	78	82	82	77	69	62	56
maximum*	°C	13	14	16	18	21	25	28	28	25	21	16	13
average daily	°F	43	45	48	52	57	65	69	69	66	58	51	46
minimum*	°C	6	7	9	11	14	18	21	21	19	15	11	8
average sea	°F	55	55	55	57	60	69	70	73	70	68	60	57
temperatures	°C	13	13	13	14	16	20	22	23	22	20	16	14

*Minimum temperatures are measured just before sunrise, maximum temperatures in the afternoon.

Planning Your Budget

To give you an idea of what to expect, here's a list of average prices in Spanish pesetas. However, they must be regarded as approximate, as inflation creeps relentlessly up. Prices quoted may be subject to a VAT/sales tax (IVA) of either 6 or 12%.

Baby-sitters. 350–400 ptas. per hour.

Camping. *De luxe:* 400–500 ptas. per day per person, 1,500–2,000 ptas. per tent or caravan (trailer). *3rd category:* 300–400 ptas. per day per person, 550–650 ptas. per tent or caravan. Reductions for children.

Car hire. *Seat Fura L* 2,750 ptas. per day, 22 ptas. per km., 33,600 ptas. per week with unlimited mileage. *Ford Escort* 3,950 ptas. per day, 35 ptas. per km., 52,000 ptas. per week with unlimited mileage. *Ford Sierra 2000* 8,200 ptas. per day, 70 ptas. per km., 112,000 ptas. per week with unlimited mileage. Add 12% IVA.

Cigarettes. Spanish brands 60–115 ptas. per packet of 20, imported brands 175 ptas. and up.

Entertainment. Cinema in Barcelona 400–450 ptas., in resorts 200–300 ptas. Theatre 500–1,200 ptas. Flamenco nightclub 700 ptas. and up. Discotheque 400 ptas. and up. Museums 175–200 ptas.

Hairdressers. *Woman's* shampoo and set or blow-dry 700–1,500 ptas. *Man's* haircut 500–1,500 ptas.

Hotels (double room with bath per night). ***** 13,000 ptas., **** 9,000 ptas., *** 6,000 ptas., ** 4,000 ptas., * 2,800 ptas. Add 12% (for luxury hotels) or 6% (for other hotels) IVA.

Meals and drinks. Continental breakfast 350–400 ptas., *plato del día* 500 ptas., lunch/dinner in a good restaurant 1,500–2,000 ptas., beer 60–80 ptas., coffee 45–55 ptas., Spanish brandy 80–200 ptas., soft drinks 80–150 ptas.

Metro. 50 ptas. (55 ptas. on Sundays and holidays).

Shopping bag. Bread (½ kg.) 50 ptas., 100 g. of butter 160 ptas., eggs 130–180 ptas., 1 kg. of veal 1,200–1,600 ptas., 250 g. of coffee 263 ptas., 1 l. of fruit juice 160 ptas., 1 l. of milk 74–90 ptas., bottle of wine from 100 ptas.

Taxi. Initial charge 200 ptas. (including the first 6 minutes or the first 2 km.) 50 ptas. per km., 40 ptas. per piece of luggage.

An A–Z Summary of Practical Information and Facts

> A star (*) following an entry indicates that relevant prices are to be found on page 101.
>
> Listed after some basic entries is the appropriate Spanish translation, usually in the singular, plus a number of phrases that should help you when seeking assistance.

A **AIRPORT** *(aeropuerto).* Barcelona's modern international airport, along the sea at El Prat de Llobregat, is only about 15 kilometres from the centre of the city. Porters are available to carry your bags to the taxi rank or bus stop; free baggage trolleys also are at passengers' disposal. A tourist information office, car hire agencies, souvenir shops, a currency exchange office and a duty-free shop operate here.

The Spanish Railways operate a link between the airport and Central-Sants station in western Barcelona. Trains run every 30 minutes, and the trip takes only 15–20 minutes.

Charter flights for resorts near Tarragona often use the military airfield at Reus. Tour operators provide ground transportation.

B **BABY-SITTERS*.** This service can usually be arranged with your hotel. Rates can vary considerably but are generally lower in the quieter resort areas; in most places they go up after midnight.

Can you get me a baby-sitter for tonight?	**¿Puede conseguirme una niñera (or, un "canguro") para esta noche?**

BICYCLE and **MOTORSCOOTER HIRE** *(bicicletas/scooters de alquiler).* In a few resorts, bicycles—including tandem models—may be hired by the hour or by the day. You may also be able to find a garage which will rent you a moped by the day or week. However, these 49-cc. machines are a less-than-carefree mode of transport on resort-area roads, especially in season when traffic is extremely heavy.

Motorscooters of 150 to 175-cc., powerful enough for a driver and a passenger, cost almost as much to hire as a car. Be prepared to lay out a deposit. Remember that use of crash helmets is compulsory, whatever the capacity of the engine.

I'd like to hire a bicycle.	**Quisiera alquilar una bicicleta.**
What's the charge per day/week?	**¿Cuánto cobran por día/semana?**

CAMPING* *(camping)*. The Costa Dorada has more officially approved campsites than any other resort area in Spain. Apply to the Federació Catalana de Campings:

Via Laietana, 59, Barcelona; tel. 317 4416

Camping grounds are divided into four categories (luxury, 1st, 2nd and 3rd class), and rates and facilities vary accordingly. All sites, however, have electricity, drinking water, toilets and showers, and are under surveillance night and day.

For a complete list of campsites throughout the whole of Spain, consult any Spanish National Tourist Office (see TOURIST INFORMATION OFFICES).

May we camp here?	**¿Podemos acampar aquí?**
We have a tent/caravan (trailer).	**Tenemos una tienda de camping/una caravana.**

CAR HIRE* *(coches de alquiler)*. See also DRIVING. There are car hire firms in the main towns and tourist resorts. You'll find many types of cars for hire, but the most common one is the Seat. Ask for any available seasonal deals.

A deposit, as well as advance payment of the estimated rental charge, is generally required, although holders of major credit cards are normally exempt from this. A VAT (sales tax) is added to the total; third-party insurance is automatically included.

Normally you must be over 21 to hire a car. You should have an International Driving Licence, but many firms accept a valid licence from your country of residence. You'll *probably* get away with the latter if stopped by the police, but there is a risk.

I'd like to rent a car (tomorrow).	**Quisiera alquilar un coche (para mañana).**
for one day/a week	**por un día/una semana**

CIGARETTES, CIGARS, TOBACCO* *(cigarrillos, puros, tabaco)*.
Spanish cigarettes can be made of strong, black tobacco *(negro)* or light
tobacco *(rubio)*. Imported foreign brands are up to three times the
price of local makes, though foreign brands produced in Spain under
licence can be cheaper than when bought at home. Locally made
cigars are cheap and reasonably good. Canary Island cigars are excellent and Cuban cigars are readily available. Pipe smokers find the
local tobacco somewhat rough.

Tabacalera S.A. is the government tobacco monopoly: they supply
their official shops, *tabacos* or *estancos,* who supply everybody else.
Cigarette shops often sell postage stamps, too.

A packet of…/A box of matches, please.	**Un paquete de…/Una caja de cerillas, por favor.**
filter-tipped	**con filtro**
without filter	**sin filtro**

CLOTHING. Whatever you wear for hot north European summers
will be fine for Barcelona. By day between July and early September
you'll be very unlucky to need a wrap, but have one handy in the
evenings. In other months, especially between November and March,
winds can sometimes blow cold, so always carry a jacket or coat. Even
in August you'll need a warm covering in the mountains. When visiting churches women no longer *have* to cover their heads, but decent
dress is certainly expected.

COMMUNICATIONS. Post offices *(correos)* are for mail and telegrams; you can't usually make telephone calls from them.

Post office hours. 9 a.m. to 1 or 2 p.m. and 4 or 5 to 6 or 7 p.m. Monday to Friday, mornings only on Saturdays. Barcelona's main post
office is open from 9 a.m. to 2 p.m. and 4 to 6 p.m. daily in summer,
9 a.m. to 9 p.m. in winter.

Mail. If you don't know in advance where you'll be staying, you can
have your mail addressed to the *Lista de Correos* (poste restante or
general delivery) in the nearest town. Take your passport to the post
office as identification and be prepared to pay a small fee for each
letter received.

Postage stamps are also on sale at tobacconists (*tabacos* or *estancos*) and often at hotel desks.

Mail boxes are yellow.

Telegrams *(telegrama)*. Telegram and post office counter services work independent hours and usually overlap. Times vary from town to town, too, but you can always send telegrams by phone—dial 3222000.

The telegraph section in the main post offices of major cities stays open 24 hours a day. If you are staying at a hotel, the receptionist can take telegrams. Telex service is also available in principal post offices.

Telephone *(teléfono)*. You can make local and international calls from public telephone booths in the street, from most hotels (often with heavy surcharges) and from some post offices. Area codes for different countries are given in the telephone directory. You'll need a supply of small change. For international direct dialling, pick up the receiver, wait for the dial tone, then dial 07, wait for a second sound and dial the country code (U.K. 44, Canada/U.S.A. 1), city code and subscriber's number.

To reverse the charges, ask for *cobro revertido*. For a personal (person-to-person) call, specify *persona a persona* (only valid for international calls).

Can you get me this number in…?	**¿Puede comunicarme con este número en…?**
Have you received any mail for…?	**¿Ha recibido correo para…?**
A stamp for this letter/postcard, please.	**Por favor, un sello para esta carta/tarjeta.**
express (special delivery)	**urgente**
airmail	**vía aérea**
registered	**certificado**
I want to send a telegram to…	**Quisiera mandar un telegrama a…**

COMPLAINTS. By law, all hotels, campsites and restaurants must have official complaint forms *(Hoja Oficial de Reclamación/Full Oficial de Reclamació)* and produce them on demand. The original of this triplicate document should be sent to the regional office of the Ministry of Tourism, one copy remains with the establishment complained against and you keep the third sheet. Merely asking for a complaint form is usually enough to resolve most matters since tourism authorities take a serious view of complaints and your host wants to keep both his reputation and his licence.

C

In the rare event of major obstruction, when it is not possible to call in the police, write directly to the Secretaría de Estado de Turismo, Sección de Inspección y Reclamaciones:

Duque de Medinaceli, 2, Madrid

New legislation has been introduced that greatly strengthens the consumer's hand. Public information offices are being set up, controls carried out, and fallacious information made punishable by law. For a tourist's needs, however, the tourist office, or in really serious cases, the police would normally be able to handle or, at least, to advise where to go.

CONSULATES *(consulado)*

Barcelona:

Canada. Via Augusta, 125; tel. 209 0634

Eire. Gran Via Carles III, 94, 10th floor; tel. 330 96 52

South Africa. Gran Via de les Corts Catalanes, 634; tel. 301 55 85

U.K.* Avinguda Diagonal, 477; tel. 322 21 51

U.S.A. Via Laietana, 33; tel. 319 95 50

Tarragona:

U.K.* Santián, 4; tel. 204 12 46

Almost all Western European countries have consulates in Barcelona. All embassies are located in Madrid.

If you run into trouble with authorities or the police, ask your consulate for advice.

CONVERTER CHARTS. For fluid and distance measures, see page 109. Spain uses the metric system.

Temperature

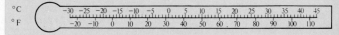

Weight

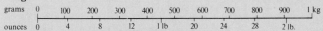

* Also for citizens of Commonwealth countries.

Length

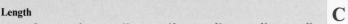

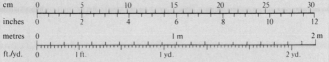

CRIME and THEFT. Spain's crime rate has caught up with the rest of the world. Thefts and break-ins are now common occurences. Hang on to purses and wallets, especially in busy places—the bullfight, open-air markets, fiestas. Don't take valuables to the beach. Lock cars and never leave cases, cameras, etc., on view. In Barcelona, tourists are a target for bag snatchers and the like—especially along the Ramblas and in the notorious Barri Chino. So be on your guard. If you suffer a theft or break-in, report it to the Guardia Civil. In Barcelona, go to your consulate where you will fill in a form that you then present at the police station *(comisaría)*.

I want to report a theft.	**Quiero denunciar un robo.**
My ticket/wallet/passport has been stolen.	**Me han robado el billete/ la cartera/el pasaporte.**

DRIVING IN SPAIN. To take your car into Spain, you should have:

● an International Driving Permit (not obligatory for citizens of most Western European countries—ask your automobile association— but recommended in case of difficulties with the police as it carries a text in Spanish) or a legalized and certified translation of your driving licence

● car registration papers

● Green Card (an extension to your regular insurance policy, making it valid for foreign countries)

Also recommended: With your certificate of insurance, you should carry a bail bond. If you injure somebody in an accident in Spain, you can be imprisoned while the accident is under investigation. This bond will bail you out. Apply to your automobile association or insurance company.

A nationality sticker must be prominently displayed on the back of your car. Seat belts are compulsory. Not using them outside towns makes you liable to a stiff fine. A red reflecting warning triangle is **107**

D compulsory when driving on motorways (expressways). Motorcycle riders and their passengers must wear crash helmets.

Driving conditions. Drive on the right. Pass on the left. Yield right of way to all traffic coming from the right. Spanish drivers tend to use their horn (daytime) or lights (night) when passing other vehicles.

Main roads are adequate to very good and improving all the time. Secondary roads can be bumpy. The main danger of driving in Spain comes from impatience, especially on busy roads. A large percentage of accidents in Spain occur when passing, so take it easy.

Spanish truck and lorry drivers will often wave you on (by hand or by flashing their right directional signal) if it's clear ahead.

Parking and driving in Barcelona, like most major cities unless you really know your way about, are not much fun. Streams of heavy traffic roar down long, straight avenues, carrying all before them (including you, probably). And beware of horrendous traffic jams on Sunday evenings as the crowds return from the beach.

Beware, too, of that delicious but oh-so-heavy Spanish wine: the drinking and driving laws have been tightened up considerably, and fines are truly horrible!

Note that on motorways in Catalonia the word for exit is *sortida,* while in the rest of Spain it is *salida*.

Speed limits: 120 k.p.h. (75 m.p.h.) on motorways, 100 k.p.h. (62 m.p.h.) or 90 k.p.h. (56 m.p.h.) on other roads, 60 k.p.h. (36 m.p.h.) in towns and built-up areas. Cars towing caravans (trailers) are restricted to 80 k.p.h. (50 m.p.h.) on the open road.

Traffic Police. The Traffic Civil Guard *(Guardia Civil de Tráfico)* patrols the highways on powerful black motorcycles. Always in pairs, these capable-looking characters are courteous, good mechanics and will stop to help anyone in trouble.

The police are, however, severe on lawbreakers. The most frequent offences include:

- speeding
- travelling too close to the car in front
- overtaking (passing) withtout flashing your direction indicator lights
- travelling at night with a burnt-out light (Spanish law requires you to carry a complete set of spare bulbs at all times)
- failing to come to a complete halt at a STOP sign

Fines are payable on the spot.

Parking. Many towns charge a token fee for parking during working hours; the cities more. The attendants are often disabled, and it's usual to round off the price of the ticket upwards.

Fuel and oil. Fuel is theoretically available in super (97 octane), normal (92 octane), unleaded (still rare; 95 octane) and diesel. But not every petrol station carries the full range. It is customary to give the attendant a coin or two as a tip.

Fluid measures

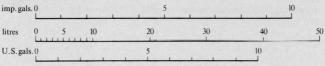

Distance

Breakdowns. Spanish garages are as efficient as any, and a breakdown will probably be cheaper to repair in Spain than in your home country. Spare parts are readily available for all major makes of cars.

Road signs. Most road signs are the standard pictographs used throughout Europe. However, you may encounter these written signs:

Aparcamiento	Parking
Autopista (de peaje/peatge)	(Toll) motorway (expressway)
Ceda el paso	Give way (Yield)
Cruce peligroso	Dangerous crossroads
Cuidado	Caution
Despacio	Slow
Desviación	Diversion (Detour)
Peligro	Danger
Prohibido adelantar	No overtaking (passing)
Prohibido aparcar	No parking
Puesto de socorro	First-aid post

(International) Driving Licence	**Carné de conducir (internacional)**
Car registration papers	**Permiso de circulación**
Green Card	**Carta verde**

109

D | Are we on the right road for...? | ¿Es ésta la carretera hacia...?
| Full tank, please. | Llene el depósito, por favor.

normal	normal
super	super
leadfree	sin plomo
Check the oil/tires/battery.	Por favor, controle el aceite/los neumáticos/la batería.
I've had a breakdown.	Mi coche se ha estropeado.
There's been an accident.	Ha habido un accidente.

DRUGS. Until the 1980s, Spain had one of the strictest drug laws in Europe. Then possession of small quantities for personal use was legalized. Now the pendulum has swung back in the other direction: possession and sale of drugs is once again a criminal offense in Spain.

E **ELECTRIC CURRENT** *(corriente eléctrica)*. Today 220-volt A.C. is becoming standard, but older installations of 125 volts can still be found. Check before plugging in. If the voltage is 125, American appliances (e.g. razors) built for 60 cycles will run on 50-cycle European current, but more slowly.

If you have trouble with any of your appliances ask your hotel receptionist to recommend an *electricista*.

| What's the voltage—125 or 220? | ¿Cuál es el voltaje—ciento veinticinco (125) o doscientos veinte (220)? |
| an adaptor/a battery | un adaptador/una pila |

EMERGENCIES. If you're not staying at a hotel, dial the police emergency number—091. You can always visit the local Municipal Police or the Guardia Civil. If possible take a Spanish speaker with you. Depending on the nature of the emergency, refer to the separate entries in this book, such as CONSULATES, MEDICAL CARE, POLICE, etc.

Though we hope you'll never need them, here are a few key words you might like to learn in advance:

Careful	Cuidado	Police	Policía
Fire	Fuego	Stop	Deténgase
110 Help	Socorro	Stop thief	Al ladrón

ENTRY and CUSTOMS FORMALITIES *(aduana)*. Most visitors require only a valid passport to visit Spain, and even this requirement is waived for the British, who may enter on the simplified Visitor's Passport. Though residents of Europe and North America aren't subject to any health requirements, visitors from further afield should check with a travel agent before departure in case inoculation certificates are called for.

The following chart shows customs allowances for certain items of personal use.

Into:	Cigarettes		Cigars		Tobacco	Spirits	Wine
Spain 1)	300	or	75	or	350 g.	1.5 l. and 5 l.	
2)	200	or	50	or	250 g.	1 l. or 2 l.	
Australia	200	or	250 g.	or	250 g.	1 l. or 1 l.	
Canada	200	and	50	and	900 g.	1.1 l. or 1.1 l.	
Eire	200	or	50	or	250 g.	1 l. and 2 l.	
N. Zealand	200	or	50	or	250 g.	1.1 l. and 4.5 l.	
S. Africa	400	and	50	and	250 g.	1 l. and 2 l.	
U.K.	200	or	50	or	250 g.	1 l. and 2 l.	
U.S.A.	200	and	100	and	3)	1 l. or 1 l.	

1) Visitors arriving from EEC countries.
2) Visitors arriving from other countries.
3) A reasonable quantity.

Currency restrictions. Tourists may bring an unlimited amount of Spanish or foreign currency into the country. Departing, though, you must declare any amount beyond the equivalent of 500,000 pesetas. Thus if you plan to carry large sums in and out again it's wise to declare your currency on arrival as well as on departure.

FIRE *(incendio)*. Forest fires are a real menace during the scorching summers in Catalonia, so be very careful where you throw your cigarette butts. If you are camping, make sure your fire is extinguished before you move.

G **GUIDES** *(guía)*. Local tourist offices, hotels and travel agencies can put you in touch with qualified guides and interpreters if you want a personally directed tour or help in business negotiations.

We'd like an English-speaking guide.	**Queremos un guía que hable inglés**
I need an English interpreter.	**Necesito un intérprete de inglés.**

H **HAIRDRESSERS*** *(peluquería)* and **BARBERS** *(barbería)*. Many hotels have their own salons, and the standard is generally good. Prices vary widely according to the class of establishment, but rates are often displayed in the window.

Not too much off (here).	**No corte mucho (aquí).**
A little more off (here).	**Un poco más (aquí).**
haircut	**corte**
shampoo and set	**lavado y marcado**
blow-dry	**modelado**
permanent wave	**permanente**
a colour rinse/hair-dye	**champú colorante/tinte**
a colour chart	**un muestrario de tintes**

HITCH-HIKING *(auto-stop)*. In Spain, hitch-hiking is permitted everywhere and is on the whole safe—which does not mean that it is necessarily easy! Waiting under that unblinking sun can be a thirsty business, interspersed with moments of despair... Best hitch-hike in pairs; girls have a better chance in this "game". If you sleep out in the open, don't bed down close to camping and caravan (trailer) sites. Police passing the campsite may awaken you to check your identity.

Can you give me/us a lift to...?	**¿Puede llevarme/llevarnos a...?**

HOTELS and ACCOMMODATION* *(hotel; alojamiento)*. Spanish hotel prices are no longer government-controlled. Accommodation ranges from simple rooms in a *pension* (boarding house) to the luxurious surroundings of a five-star hotel. Before the guest takes the room he fills out a form indicating the hotel category, room number, price and signs it. Breakfast is normally included in the room rate.

When you check into your hotel you might have to leave your passport at the desk. Don't worry, you'll get it back in the morning.

Other accommodation:

Hostal and **Hotel-Residencia:** Modest hotels, often family concerns, also graded by stars.

Pensión. Boarding house, few amenities.

Fonda. Village inn, clean and unpretentious.

Parador. State-run inns, often in beautifully restored old buildings and often in isolated or little developed areas.

Albergue de Juventud. There are youth hostels in Arenys de Mar, Barcelona and Tarragona. During the tourist season it is wise to book in advance.

a single/double room	**una habitación individual/ doble**
with bath/shower	**con baño/ducha**
What's the rate per night?	**¿Cuál es el precio por noche?**

HOURS. To accommodate the midday pause, most shops and offices open from 9 a.m. to 2 p.m. and then from 4 p.m. to 8 p.m. or later. Restaurants start serving lunch about 1 p.m. and dinner between 8 and 10 p.m.

LANGUAGE. The official language of Spain, Castilian, is understood in Barcelona and on the Costa Dorada. However, a related Romance language, Catalan, is the native language of the people of Catalonia. Since the death of General Franco, there has been an immense increase in the use of Catalan and many Catalans express themselves more freely—and more willingly—in Catalan than in Spanish. On a brief visit to Barcelona and the Costa Dorada, your elementary Spanish will suffice, even if a few words of Catalan will always be appreciated.

For geographical reasons, the French language is widely understood and admired in Catalonia. In tourist areas, English and German are spoken as well. See also MAPS AND STREET NAMES.

L

	Catalan	Castilian
Good morning	*Bon dia*	*Buenos días*
Good afternoon	*Bona tarda*	*Buenas tardes*
Good night	*Bona nit*	*Buenas noches*
Thank you	*Gràcies*	*Gracias*
You're welcome	*De res*	*De nada*
Please	*Si us plau*	*Por favor*
Goodbye	*Adéu*	*Adiós*

The Berlitz phrase book SPANISH FOR TRAVELLERS covers most situations you are likely to encounter during your travels in Spain. The Berlitz Spanish-English/English-Spanish pocket dictionary contains 12,500 concepts, plus a menu-reader supplement.

Do you speak English?	**¿Habla usted inglés?**
I don't speak Spanish.	**No hablo español.**

LAUNDRY *(lavandería)* and **DRY-CLEANING** *(tintorería)*. Most hotels will handle laundry and dry-cleaning, but they'll usually charge more than a laundry or a dry-cleaners. For still greater savings, you can try a *quick service*.

Wher's the nearest laundry/dry-cleaners?	**¿Dónde está la lavandería/ tintorería más cercana?**
When will it be ready?	**¿Cuándo estará listo?**
I must have this for tomorrow morning.	**Lo necesito para mañana por la mañana.**

LOST PROPERTY. The first thing to do when you discover you've lost something is, obviously, to retrace your steps. If nothing comes to light, report the loss to the Municipal Police or the Guardia Civil.

I've lost my wallet/handbag/ passport.	**He perdido mi cartera/bolso/ pasaporte.**

M **MAPS and STREET NAMES.** Spain has been undergoing a formidable upheaval in many domains since 1975. One manifestation is in the names of streets, many of which are being re-baptised, causing a tourist considerable confusion.

Place and street names in Catalonia are mostly met with today in their Catalan version: former San Carlos is now seen as Sant Carles, Lérida as Lleida, Gerona as Girona, etc.

A tip to help recognize Catalan street signs:

Castilian	English	Catalan
Avenida	Avenue	*Avinguda*
Calle	Street	*Carrer*
Iglesia	Church	*Església*
Palacio	Palace	*Palau*
Paseo	Boulevard	*Passeig*
Pasaje	Passageway	*Passatge*
Plaza	Square	*Plaça*

The maps in this book were prepared by Falk-Verlag, Hamburg, that also publish a detailed map of Barcelona.

I'd like a street plan of…	**Quisiera un plano de la ciudad de…**
a road map of this region	**un mapa de carreteras de esta comarca**

MEDICAL CARE. By far the best solution, to be completely at ease, is to take out a special health insurance policy to cover the risk of illness and accident while on holiday. Your travel agent can also fix you up with Spanish tourist insurance (ASTES), but it is a slow-moving process. ASTES covers doctors' fees and clinical care.

Health care in the resort areas and in the major cities is good but expensive, hence the need for adequate insurance. Most of the major resort towns have private clinics; the cities and rural areas are served by municipal or provincial hospitals.

For minor ailments, visit the local first-aid post *(casa de socorro* or *dispensario).* Away from your hotel, don't hesitate to ask the police or a tourist information office for help. At your hotel, ask the staff to help you.

Pharmacies *(farmacia)* are usually open during normal shopping hours. After hours, at least one per town remains open all night, the *farmacia de guardia.* Its location is posted in the window of all other *farmacias.*

Where's the nearest (all-night) pharmacy?	**¿Dónde está la farmacia (de guardia) más cercana?**
I need a doctor/dentist.	**Necesito un médico/dentista.**
I've a pain here.	**Me duele aquí.**
a fever/sunburn	**fiebre/quemadura del sol**
an upset stomach	**molestias de estómago**

M **MEETING PEOPLE.** Politeness and simple courtesies still matter in Spain. A handshake on greeting and leaving is normal. Always begin any conversation, whether with a friend, shop girl, taxi-driver, policeman or telephone operator with a *buenos días* (good morning) or *buenas tardes* (good afternoon). Always say *adiós* (good-bye) or, at night, *buenas noches* when leaving. *Por favor* (please) should begin all requests.

Incidentally if anyone should say *adiós* to you when seeing you in the street, it's not that they don't want to have anything to do with you—it's a familiar greeting, meaning roughly "hello".

The Spanish have their own pace. Not only is it bad manners to try to rush them, but unproductive as well.

MONEY MATTERS

Currency. The monetary unit of Spain is the *peseta* (abbreviated *pta.*).
Coins: 1, 2, 5, 10, 25, 50, 100, 200 pesetas.
Banknotes: 100, 200, 500, 1,000, 2,000, 5,000, 10,000 pesetas.
A 5-peseta coin is traditionally called a *duro*, so if someone should quote a price as 10 duros, he means 50 pesetas. For currency restrictions, see ENTRY AND CUSTOMS FORMALITIES.

Banking hours are from 9 a.m. to 2 p.m. Monday to Friday, till 1 p.m. on Saturdays.

Banks are closed on Sundays and holidays—watch out, too, for those local holidays which always seem to crop up in Spain! Outside normal banking hours, many travel agencies and other businesses displaying a *cambio* sign will change foreign currency into pesetas. In Barcelona, there are exchange offices open in the afternoon and on weekends at the Estació Central-Sants, Estació de França and at the airport. Both banks and exchange offices pay slightly more for traveller's cheques than for cash. Always take your passport with you when you go to exchange money.

Credit cards. All the internationally recognized cards are accepted by hotels, restaurants and businesses in Spain.

Eurocheques. You'll have no problem settling bills or paying for purchases with Eurocheques.

Traveller's cheques. In tourist areas, shops and all banks, hotels and
116 travel agencies accept them, though you're likely to get a better

exchange rate at a national or regional bank. Remember always to take your passport with you if you expect to cash a traveller's cheque.

Paying cash. Although many shops and bars will accept payment in sterling or dollars, you're better off paying in pesetas. Shops will invariably give you less than the bank rate for foreign currency.

Prices. Although Spain has by no means escaped the scourge of inflation, Barcelona remains quite competitive with the other tourist regions of Europe. An exciting night on the town—either at a discotheque or a flamenco nightclub—won't completely ruin you. In the realm of eating, drinking and smoking, Spain still provides indisputable value for money.

Certain rates are listed on page 101 to give you an idea of what things cost.

Where's the nearest bank/ currency exchange office?	¿Dónde está el banco/la oficina de cambio más cercana?
I want to change some pounds/ dollars.	Quiero cambiar libras/dólares.
Do you accept traveller's cheques?	¿Acepta usted cheques de viaje?
Can I pay with this credit card?	¿Puedo pagar con esta tarjeta de crédito?
How much is that?	¿Cuánto es?

MOSQUITOES. With the occasional exception there are rarely more than a few mosquitoes at a given time, but they survive the year round, and just one can ruin a night's sleep. Few hotels, flats or villas—anywhere on the Mediterranean—have mosquito-proofed windows. Bring your own anti-mosquito devices, whether nets, buzzers, lotions, sprays or incense-type coils that burn all night.

NEWSPAPERS and MAGAZINES *(periódico; revista).* At the height of the tourist season, all major British and Continental newspapers are on sale up and down the coast on their publication day. U.S. magazines and the Paris-based *International Herald Tribune* are also available.

Have you any English-language newspapers/magazines?	¿Tienen periódicos/revistas en inglés?

P **PHOTOGRAPHY.** There's tremendous scope for the keen photographer, but beware of the light. For beaches, whitewashed houses and other strongly lit scenes, use incidental readings stopped down, i.e. reduced by one-third or one-half stop; or follow the instructions with the film. If in doubt, bracket your exposures—expose above and below the selected exposure—especially with transparency film. For good results don't shoot between 11 a.m. and 3 p.m. unless there's light cloud to soften the sun.

All popular brands and most sizes of film (except 220) are available. Imported films and chemicals are expensive, so bring as much as you can with you.

Spanish-made film is much less expensive and of a reasonable quality. To get best results from the black-and-white *Negra* and *Valca*, you'll need to experiment, especially with processing. The colour negative film *Negracolor* is fine for family shots. All transparency film is imported.

Shops in Barcelona and major resorts can develop and print black-and-white or colour film in a few days, and some specialize in 1-hour service. If possible always keep film—exposed and unexposed—in a refrigerator.

Photos shops sell lead-coated plastic bags which protect films from X-rays at airport security checkpoints.

I'd like a film for this camera.	**Quisiera un carrete para esta máquina.**
a black-and-white film	**un carrete en blanco y negro**
a colour-slide film	**un carrete de diapositivas**
a film for colour-pictures	**un carrete para película en color**
35-mm film	**un carrete treinta y cinco**
super-8	**super ocho**
How long will it take to develop (and print) this film?	**¿Cuánto tardará en revelar (y sacar copias de) este carrete?**

POLICE *(policía).* There are three police forces in Spain: the *Policía Municipal,* who are attached to the local town hall and usually wear a blue uniform; the *Cuerpo Nacional de Policía,* a national anti-crime unit recognized by their blue-and-white uniforms; and the *Guardia Civil,* the national police force patrolling highways and rural areas.

If you need police assistance, you can call on any one of the three.

Where's the nearest police station?	**¿Dónde está la comisaría más cercana?**

PUBLIC HOLIDAYS *(fiesta)*

January 1	*Año Nuevo*	New Year's Day
January 6	*Epifanía*	Epiphany
March 19	*San José*	St. Joseph's Day
May 1	*Día del Trabajo*	Labour Day
July 25	*Santiago Apóstol*	St. James's Day
August 15	*Asunción*	Assumption
October 12	*Día de la Hispanidad*	Discovery of America Day (Columbus Day)
November 1	*Todos los Santos*	All Saints' Day
December 6	*Día de la Constitución Española*	Constitution Day
December 25	*Navidad*	Christmas Day
Movable dates:	*Jueves Santo*	Maundy Thursday
	Viernes Santo	Good Friday
	Lunes de Pascua	Easter Monday (Catalonia only)
	Corpus Christi	Corpus Christi
	Inmaculada Concepción	Immaculate Conception (normally December 8)

These are only the national holidays of Spain. There are many special holidays for different branches of the economy or different regions. Consult the tourist office where you are staying.

Are you open tomorrow?   **¿Está abierto mañana?**

RADIO and TV *(radio; televisión)*. A short-wave set of reasonable quality will pick up all European capitals. Reception of Britain's BBC World Service usually rates from good to excellent, either direct or through their eastern Mediterranean relay station. In the winter, especially mornings and evenings, a good set will pull in the BBC medium and long wave "home" programmes. The Voice of America usually comes through loud and clear, though in Spain the programme is not received 24 hours a day. The Spanish music programme, *segundo programa*, jazz to Bach but mostly classical, is excellent. It's FM only, around 88 UKW on the band.

R   Most hotels and bars have television, usually tuned in to sports—including international soccer and rugby—bull fighting, variety or nature programmes.

RELIGIOUS SERVICES *(servicio religioso)*. The national religion of Spain is Roman Catholic. Masses are said regularly in almost all churches, including those of outstanding artistic or historical interest.

In Barcelona, Catholic and Protestant services are held in foreign languages, and there is also a synagogue and a mosque. In Barcelona Cathedral, confessions are heard each Sunday in English.

T   **TIME DIFFERENCES.** Spanish time coincides with most of Western Europe—Greenwich Mean Time plus one hour. In spring, another hour is added for Daylight Saving Time (Summer Time).

Summer Time chart:

New York	London	**Spain**	Jo'burg	Sydney	Auckland
6 a.m.	11 a.m.	**noon**	noon	8 p.m.	10 p.m.

What time is it?   **¿Qué hora es?**

TIPPING. Since a service charge is normally included in hotel and restaurant bills, tipping is not obligatory. However, it's appropriate to tip porters, bellboys, etc., for their efforts. Follow the chart below for rough guidelines.

Hotel porter, per bag	50 ptas.
Maid, for extra services	100–200 ptas.
Waiter	10% (optional)
Taxi driver	10%
Tourist guide	10%
Hairdresser	10%
Lavatory attendant	25–50 ptas.

TOILETS. There are many expressions for "toilets" in Spanish: *aseos, servicios., W.C., water* and *retretes.* The first terms are the more common.

Public toilets are to be found in most large towns, but rarely in villages. However, just about every bar and restaurant has a toilet available for public use. It's considered polite to buy a coffee or a glass of wine if you drop in specifically to use the conveniences.

Where are the toilets? **¿Dónde están los servicios?**

TOURIST INFORMATION OFFICES *(oficinas de turismo).* Spanish National Tourist Offices are maintained in many countries throughout the world:

Canada. 60 Bloor St. West, Suite 201, Toronto, Ont. M4W-3B8; tel. (416) 961-3131

United Kingdom. 57–58, St. James's St., London SW1 A1LD; tel. (01) 499-0901.

U.S.A. 845 N. Michigan Ave., Chicago, IL 60611; tel. (312) 944-0215.

8383 Wilshire Blvd., Suite 960, Beverly Hills, CA 90211; tel. (213) 658-7188/93.

4800 The Galleria, 5085 Westheimer Rd., Houston, TX 77056; tel. (713) 840-7411.

665 5th Ave., New York, NY 10022; tel. (212) 759-8822.

Casa del Hidalgo, Hypolita & St. George Streets, St. Augustine, FL 31084; tel. (904) 829-6460.

These offices will supply you with a wide range of colourful and informative brochures and maps in English on the various towns and regions in Spain. They will also let you consult a copy of the master directory of hotels in Spain, listing all facilities and prices.

All major cities and leading resorts in Spain have their own tourist information offices, all of which will be delighted to provide information and brochures on local tourist attractions.

Barcelona: At the airport, the central railway station (Estació Central-Sants), the Estació de França (in the harbour), in Plaça de Sant Jaume (Gothic Quarter) and in Gran Via de les Corts Catalanes, 658.

Barcelona's tourist authority is the Patronat Municipal de Turisme, Passeig de Gràcia 35, 08007 Barcelona.

While in Barcelona, you can dial 010 for tourist and other information about the city.

Sitges: Plaça d'Eduard Maristany

Tarragona: Rambla Nova, 46

Where is the tourist office? **¿Dónde está la oficina de turismo?** 121

T TRANSPORT

Buses. More than 50 bus lines cover Barcelona. As in many cities, the rush hours are best avoided.

Buses are boarded from the front, and tickets are issued by the driver. Take out a multiple-journey ticket valid for bus and Metro if it looks likely you're going to travel around and sightsee a lot in Barcelona. A simple and excellent way to sightsee is to hop on—or off, as many times and wherever you like—bus No. 100—all on the same ticket. The route followed in a 1½-hour tour takes in the most interesting highspots of a Barcelona visit. Departure from Pla del Palau every 45 minutes.

To reach the resorts from Barcelona, trains are more frequent and practical than the bus services.

Metro*. Barcelona's underground railway, consisting of five main lines, criss-crosses the city more rapidly than other forms of public transport.

"Metro" signs with a red diamond-shaped insignia mark the entrances where detailed maps of all lines are displayed. Trains run from 5 a.m. to 11 p.m.

Taxis*. You can recognize taxis by the letters SP *(servicio público)* on the front and rear bumpers. They may also have a green light on the roof and a *libre* (free) sign on the windscreen. Each town has its own type of car and colour scheme (Barcelona's taxis are all painted yellow and black). In smaller towns, there are fixed fares instead of meters; in major cities, the meter clicks relentlessly as you go. The figure displayed at the end of your trip probably is not the full fare— the driver carries an official list giving the correct total, adjusted upwards for inflation. Additional charges are legitimately made for any number of circumstances—such as nights and holidays, or picking you up at a railway station, airport, theatre or bullring. Whatever the total, it usually still costs less than a comparable journey in many other European countries.

Ferries. From Barcelona, there are regular ferry services (with cabin or deck seating) to Palma de Mallorca, Menorca and Ibiza. For information and booking, contact any local travel agency.

Trains. From Barcelona, main line trains reach to most corners of Spain. Local trains are slow, stopping at most stations. Long-distance services are fast and punctual. Tickets can be purchased at travel agencies as well as at the stations *(estació[n] de ferrocarril)*. For bargain rail tickets, see p. 100.

Trains to resorts north-east of Barcelona use the Cercanías station, a separate installation behind the Estació de França in the harbour. Suburban trains to the south-east run from the Passeig de Gràcia station in the centre of town and from the central station—Estació de Sants—in western Barcelona.

EuroCity (EC)	International express, first and second classes
Talgo, Intercity, Electrotren, Ter, Tren Estrella	Luxury, first and second classes; supplementary charge over regular fare
Expreso, Rápido	Long-distance expresses, stopping at main stations only; supplementary charge
Omnibus, Tranvía, Automotor	Local trains, with frequent stops, usually second class only
Auto Expreso	Car train
coche cama	Sleeping-car with 1-, 2- or 3-bed compartments, washing facilities
coche comedor	Dining-car
litera	Sleeping-berth car *(couchette)* with blankets, sheets and pillows
furgón de equipajes	Luggage van (baggage car); only registered luggage permitted

When's the next bus/train to…?	**¿Cuándo sale el próximo autobús/ tren para…?**
single (one-way)	**ida**
return (round-trip)	**ida y vuelta**
What's the fare to…?	**¿Cuánto es la tarifa a…?**
first/second class	**primera/segunda clase**
I'd like to make seat reservations.	**Quiero reservar asientos.**
Where can I get a taxi?	**¿Dónde puedo coger un taxi?**

W

WATER. If you're particularly sensitive to a change in water, you may want to order the bottled variety. Both still (non-carbonated) and fizzy (carbonated) water are available.

a bottle of mineral water	**una botella de agua mineral**
fizzy (carbonated)	**con gas**
still (non-carbonated)	**sin gas**
Is this drinking water?	**¿El agua es potable?**

DAYS OF THE WEEK

Sunday	**domingo**	Thursday	**jueves**
Monday	**lunes**	Friday	**viernes**
Tuesday	**martes**	Saturday	**sábado**
Wednesday	**miércoles**		

NUMBERS

0	**cero**	18	**dieciocho**
1	**uno**	19	**diecinueve**
2	**dos**	20	**veinte**
3	**tres**	21	**veintiuno**
4	**cuatro**	22	**veintidós**
5	**cinco**	30	**treinta**
6	**seis**	31	**treinta y uno**
7	**siete**	32	**treinta y dos**
8	**ocho**	40	**cuarenta**
9	**nueve**	50	**cincuenta**
10	**diez**	60	**sesenta**
11	**once**	70	**setenta**
12	**doce**	80	**ochenta**
13	**trece**	90	**noventa**
14	**catorce**	100	**cien**
15	**quince**	101	**cientouno**
16	**dieciséis**	500	**quinientos**
17	**diecisiete**	1,000	**mil**

SOME USEFUL EXPRESSIONS

yes/no	sí/no
please/thank you	por favor/gracias
excuse me/you're welcome	perdone/de nada
where/when/how	dónde/cuándo/cómo
how long/how far	cuánto tiempo/a qué distancia
yesterday/today/tomorrow	ayer/hoy/mañana
day/week/month/year	día/semana/mes/año
left/right	izquierda/derecha
up/down	arriba/abajo
good/bad	bueno/malo
big/small	grande/pequeño
cheap/expensive	barato/caro
hot/cold	caliente/frío
old/new	viejo/nuevo
open/closed	abierto/cerrado
here/there	aquí/allí
free (vacant)/occupied	libre/ocupado
early/late	temprano/tarde
easy/difficult	fácil/difícil

Does anyone here speak English?	¿Hay alguien aquí que hable inglés?
What does this mean?	¿Qué quiere decir esto?
I don't understand.	No comprendo.
Please write it down.	Escríbamelo, por favor.
Is there an admission charge?	¿Se debe pagar la entrada?
Waiter!/Waitress!	¡Camarero!/¡Camarera!
I'd like…	Quisiera…
How much is that?	¿Cuánto es?
Have you something less expensive?	¿Tiene algo más barato?
Just a minute.	Un momento.
Help me, please.	Ayúdeme, por favor.
Get a doctor, quickly.	¡Llamen a un médico, rápidamente!

Index

088/811 RPC 2